the party book

the party book

hamlyn

This edition first published in the U.K. in 1999 by
Hamlyn, a division of Octopus Publishing Group Limited
2–4 Heron Quays, London E14 4JP

Reprinted 2001

ISBN 0 600 60556 6

Printed in Hong Kong

The publisher would like to thank Anne Johnson for writing the main text for this book.

NOTES
Both metric and imperial measurements have been given in all recipes. Use one set of measurements only, and not a mixture of both.

Standard level spoon measurements are used in all recipes.
1 tablespoon = one 15 ml spoon
1 teaspoon = one 5 ml spoon

The measure that has been used in the cocktail recipes is based on a bar jigger, which is 45 ml/1½ fl oz. If preferred, a different volume can be used providing the proportions are kept constant within a drink and suitable adjustments are made to spoon measurements, where they occur.

Eggs should be medium to large unless otherwise stated. The Department of Health advises that eggs should not be consumed raw. This book contains dishes made with raw or lightly cooked eggs. It is prudent for more vulnerable people such as pregnant and nursing mothers, invalids, the elderly, babies and young children to avoid uncooked or lightly cooked dishes made with eggs. Once prepared, these dishes should be kept refrigerated and used promptly.

Meat and poultry should be cooked thoroughly. To test if poultry is cooked, pierce the flesh through the thickest part with a skewer or fork — the juices should run clear, never pink or red. Do not re-freeze poultry that has been frozen previously and thawed.

Do not re-freeze a cooked dish that has been frozen previously.

Milk should be full fat unless otherwise stated.

Nut and Nut Derivatives
This book includes dishes made with nuts and nut derivatives. It is advisable for customers with known allergic reactions to nuts and nut derivatives and those who may be potentially vulnerable to these allergies, such as pregnant and nursing mothers, invalids, the elderly, babies and children, to avoid dishes made with nuts and nut oils. It is also prudent to check the labels of pre-prepared ingredients for the possible inclusion of nut derivatives.

Pepper should be freshly ground black pepper unless otherwise stated.

Fresh herbs should be used, unless otherwise stated. If unavailable, use dried herbs as an alternative, but halve the quantities stated.

Measurements for canned food have been given as a standard metric equivalent.

Ovens should be pre-heated to the specified temperature — if using a fan-assisted oven, follow the manufacturer's instructions for adjusting the time and the temperature.

Vegetarians should look for the 'V' symbol on a cheese to ensure it is made with vegetarian rennet. There are vegetarian forms of Parmesan, feta, Cheddar, Cheshire, Red Leicester, dolcelatte and many goats' cheeses, among others.

Contents

Introduction   6

Initial Planning   14

Invitations   28

Setting the Scene   38

Entertainment   84

Liquid Refreshments   98

   Drinks   126

Party Food   148

   Finger Food   170

   Fork Food   196

   Sit Down Meals   220

The Perfect Host   246

Index   252

Introduction

Parties are all about celebration. A group of people who have got together to enjoy some delicious food and plentiful drink is reason enough for celebration.

Our eating habits have become less formal these days, and the trend is for more frequent and more intimate parties. Parties recharge the social batteries, and the desire to entertain friends and family – be it a few people around the kitchen table or a grand buffet party for a crowd – is very much alive and well. No doubt we all hope that the compliment will soon be returned. Above all, parties are meant to be enjoyed – and that goes for the host and hostess as well as all the guests.

People have been giving parties since time immemorial. Any browse through literature over the years will find people partying for any number of reasons – coming of age, Christmas, graduation, being promoted to the rank of officer, winning a war, marriage between two people eager to plight their troth, the birth of a baby – all those milestones, small and large, that crop up from time to time throughout a person's life and deserve to be recognized, or commemorated, in some way. You name it, and you will find that people have always thrown a party for it.

In this country we have always had a reputation for giving parties at the drop of a hat. The slightest reason is good enough. In the words of Douglas Jerrold, the nineteenth-century dramatist and wit: 'If an earthquake were to engulf England tomorrow, the English would manage to meet and dine somewhere among the rubbish, just to celebrate the event.' And he was absolutely right.

But it's not just the English. People give parties the world over: rich and poor, young and old. There are absolutely no essential prerequisites to throwing a party. You don't even need a house because, when the weather's good, the street will do just as well. All anyone needs is the will to get it together, the time to spare and the determination to succeed. The rest should follow naturally.

But deciding to have a party is only the first step and there are many things other than that which need to be considered.

Exactly what is it that you're wanting to celebrate – if anything? This can vary dramatically. You may, for example, be celebrating a special time of the year, such as Christmas or New Year, perhaps. Or maybe, a little later in the year, it might be Easter or Midsummer's Day. In the case of major festivities of this kind, which come round with reassuring regularity, there will never be any shortage of eager people who would like nothing more than to celebrate with you.

Or perhaps you are celebrating a private event, such as a wedding anniversary, a birthday, a friend's home-coming from distant travels, an engagement party for young lovers, or a house-warming, in which case the joy of the occasion is precisely that it is such a very personal celebration – a special occasion for a special person.

But you don't actually need to have an excuse to throw a party. It can simply happen, and there's absolutely nothing to stop you celebrating just for the hell of it. You may just want to get together with a group of friends, for example, or perhaps with some neighbours or colleagues. Maybe the weather's been glorious and a barbecue in the garden suddenly seems like the perfect idea, in which case you're not celebrating anything in particular – other than life, the weather, friendship and the gathering together of a few people who get on well.

A Success

But whatever the reason for people to gather together, above all you want the occasion to be a success. That doesn't mean, however, that it's got to be the most successful party ever held. Nor does it have to be the wildest, zaniest, biggest, most expensive, loudest or most stylish party – in fact it doesn't have to be the most anything because, quite simply, not everyone wants that. Some people just prefer things to be simple, quietly discreet, low-key, casual.

But there's no question about it – whatever you choose to do and however you choose to do it, it has to be good. The most important thing, let's face it – is the intention of having fun, but what exactly does that mean? Fun is a very personal thing and everyone has a completely different idea of what it is. In other words, it just has to work for you and your particular guests – whoever they might be, however old they are, however many of them there are, and whatever they want. The trick is

'The guests are met, the feast is set
May'st hear the merry din.'

Samuel Taylor Coleridge (1772–1834)

to have the sensitivity to know exactly what is right for you and your guests. That may sound like a patronising thing to say, and you may think it is rather stating the obvious and that you will of course know what will be acceptable and enjoyable, but it's surprising, when it comes down to it, how many people manage to get this bit utterly wrong.

You need to think long and hard about what sort of party your friends would like. What sort of people are they? If you want to invite a mixed bunch of people, what can you do to make sure that the party will appeal to everyone?

Just as there's no sense in ordering dozens of cases of booze and inviting a group of teetotallers, so there's no point in roasting several joints of expensive, well-hung meat and then inviting vegetarians, or hiring a karaoke for a party of very serious middle-aged mothers who'd much rather talk about fund-raising for the local school. So the first thing is to think about what sort of people you are inviting and what they would really enjoy.

Gathered Here Together . . .

A social gathering with good friends is fun. This is always so, whatever the occasion – be it an unexpected meeting with old chums, an impromptu supper party, a big family get-together, or a large buffet party designed to mark the dawn of a new year. Whatever the reason – and no matter how large or small, formal or informal, glamorous or simple, expensive or thrifty – any party is meant to be a highly enjoyable event for all concerned. And provided that you invite the right people and serve the right food and drink, it simply can't

fail. Or can it? It isn't always as simple as that – everyone's been to a disastrous party where everything seems to go wrong. To spend all that time, effort and money throwing a party that no one enjoys is about as close to social hell on earth as you can get, so what can you do to avoid it?

Yet everyone loves going to a party. The anticipation starts the moment the invitation drops through the letterbox and continues with the acceptance of the invitation, making that all-important decision about what to wear, the purchase of a bunch of flowers or a bottle of wine to take along, culminating in eventual arrival at the appointed house. The high point is probably when you take a sip of that first glass of wine and look forward to the party ahead, in a warm glow of happy expectation.

Throwing a Party

But still more satisfying than going to a good party is giving one yourself. There's something really special about throwing open the doors to your home – which is usually your own private space – and inviting friends in to join you. Being in control and making sure that everyone has a good time is a lot harder work than going to someone else's party, and, needless to say, it's also a much bigger strain. However, giving a party is also much more of a challenge – and, as a result, much more rewarding. Being able to look back on a really good evening, sure in the knowledge that you were responsible for its great success, gives you a warm glow – a truly fantastic feeling of satisfaction.

Throwing a party is tremendous fun, but it can also be a major headache. There are so many things you have to do. There are all those little things that you have to remember, and the

things that can go wrong – and all too soon it can quickly turn into a nightmare. Not that this happens very often, admittedly, but the possibility is always there, at the back of your mind, and there are very few people who manage to throw a party without experiencing a few misgivings.

Just think about all the anxieties that are likely to beset you before any of your guests turn up. What if no one comes? What if you forget to take the dessert out of the freezer in time? What if the meat isn't cooked properly? What if the avocados are black? What if they don't like fish? What if the pudding isn't sweet enough? What if no one likes liver? What if the soufflé doesn't rise? What if there isn't enough ice cream? What if the wine runs out? What if someone's allergic to the cats? What if Jerry and Bob hate each other at first sight and they end up having a fight? What if, what if, what if . . . Oh God . . . who hasn't felt like that just before their party begins. But, that said, everything usually goes according to plan, most parties are a lot of fun and disaster doesn't generally strike. There are, anyway, a number of ways of ensuring that your party is a success other than resorting to reading tea leaves and prayer.

And this is where *The Party Book* comes in. What this book aims to do is to help you increase the fun in party giving, to decrease the headache and to ensure success every time.

Initial Planning

The first – and probably the most important – piece of advice that anyone can give you is that a good party needs careful forethought. The secret of success in party-giving is careful, forward planning and good organization – right down to the last detail. Remember that cooking

> *'If an earthquake were to engulf England tomorrow, the English would manage to meet and dine somewhere among the rubbish, just to celebrate the event.'*

Douglas Jerrold (1803–1857)

for a lot of people takes up a great deal of time and space – from the shopping to the cooking, from laying the table to the washing up – so be well prepared.

In Chapter 1, you'll find out all the things you need to think about and how to achieve success by making lists and catering for every eventuality. It is this that ensures that a party goes to plan, with a seemingly effortless swing. Above all, it is important, too, never to cross your fingers and hope for the best and never to take anything for granted.

The hosts' aim of giving their guests a thoroughly good time is not an easy one to fulfil. The good host or hostess is a relaxed one, and this is only possible if he or she feels sufficiently at ease to enjoy the party as much as the guests do.

Invitations

Compiling your guest list is an important preliminary step, and there is useful advice in these pages on how to do this. Issuing invitations is perhaps one of the most pleasurable parts of giving a party – it's all fun without any of the hard work – and it gets people in the mood. Find out, too, how it's best to issue your invitations – whether by telephone or in writing – and when you should give your friends ample advance warning, as well as how to deal with the replies.

Setting the Scene

Parties are all about celebration, which is why it's so important to set the scene and to give everyone the message 'party' as soon as they come through your front door. The trick,

though, is to do it without it being too obvious. However wonderful the food may be, no guest is going to feel relaxed and happy if they see their hosts rushing around the house like a pair of scalded cats. The best party gives the impression of being effortless, natural, easy – and not something that's taken you hours – days, even – of hard work behind the scenes. So, give yourself the time to create a pleasant atmosphere for your guests, and then you can relax and enjoy their company.

There are many ways of creating a party atmosphere, none of which is complicated or expensive – it is often the simplest things that say 'party' the loudest. This chapter looks at ways of getting your home ready, including tips on arranging the furniture, decorating and lighting the room, and laying the table – whether for a small dinner party or a large-scale buffet. There are ideas, too, for various theme parties, which are very fashionable these days, including a 20s Cocktail Party, an Oriental Buffet, a Mexican Dinner Party, a Midsummer Tea Party and a Sea World Dinner Party.

Entertainment

For many people, good company is the only thing needed for a party to go with a swing, apart, perhaps, from the food and drink. For others no party is complete without music, either background music or a discotheque or live band to encourage people to dance. And for still others, there needs to be organized entertainment, such as an entertainer or games – perhaps to tie in with the theme of the party.

Liquid Refreshment

Some parties can be held with little or no food and can still be a memorable success, but none can be held that will be worth remembering with little or no drink. So whatever you're serving at your party – be it a few chilled beers, an exotic fruit punch, a well-chosen wine or a cup of tea – it is important to realize that the drinks that you offer your guests deserve just as much attention as the food. Your drinks will probably be dictated by two separate but equally important things: first, the type of party you are giving; and second, the drinking patterns of your guests, which will probably be influenced by their age, temperament and social habits. This chapter gives advice on choosing, storing and serving wine and, for those who prefer a wider choice of drinks, there is also advice on apéritifs and digestifs, as well as on stocking and running a full bar. There is information, too, about cocktails, plus easy-to-follow recipes on pages 126–147 for making a few all-time favourites.

The Food

Whatever sort of party you're giving, be it a buffet party or a dinner party, it's important both to tailor the food to the occasion and to plan a balanced menu, which means not serving too much of any one thing and being careful about the overall spread of different ingredients, flavours, colours, temperatures, textures and even shapes. Think carefully, too, about the logistics: how are you going to cook,

*'Take a deep breath,
pluck up the courage
and just get on with it.'*

store or reheat all the food you're planning? Do you have enough space and do you have large enough saucepans? Do you have the space on your cooker or in your oven to cope with preparing all these separate courses? And do you have enough dishes and plates for serving them all?

No one's saying it's easy, but don't for one moment think that what you're planning has to involve you in days of anxious preparation. The aim of this book is to make entertaining as effortless as possible. Guidelines on advance preparation, cooking ahead and keeping a well-stocked freezer and a well-stocked store cupboard are all good rules to follow, and there's nothing wrong – if you are at work all day or you have a hectic family life – with cutting a few corners. That doesn't mean sending the kids out for greasy hamburgers from your local takeaway – it just means being thoughtful and imaginative and finding acceptable alternatives to hard work. You might choose to buy bags of ready-washed salad leaves, for example, rather than spending ages washing, spinning, drying and trimming them yourself; or you might use ready-prepared bottles of salad dressing and add a 'homemade' touch with chopped herbs, strips of roasted peppers and olives; or you might serve a huge pile of fresh grapes or delectable strawberries on a cake-stand, accompanied by a big bowl of whipped cream, for example, or a large cheeseboard, instead of spending hours (which you can ill afford) making a series of lavish and impressive desserts.

There is also useful advice on sticking to a rigorous timetable, which will help you get everything ready on time, leaving you prepared and relaxed when you open the front door and welcome your guests with a beaming smile. There are menu suggestions for every type of party, whether a formal dinner, a few drinks or a fun picnic, and handy tips on presentation and garnishes will help you get everything looking absolutely spot on. And there are also over 70 pages of delicious recipes to suit every occasion and every timetable, which will ensure that your party goes with a swing.

The Perfect Host

We all want to be the perfect host or hostess and everyone has their own personal picture of this paragon of social virtues. Unfortunately, however, few of us manage to be a model of supreme excellence, though most of us are still capable of throwing a successful and memorable party.

The perfect host wants his or her guests to eat well, to feel comfortable and at their ease all evening, right from the beginning, to experience pleasure in meeting the other guests that have been invited, to eat and drink their fill and more, and, above all, to enjoy themselves thoroughly. This chapter gives you sound advice on avoiding every possible disaster, plus useful tips and handy hints on dealing with some tricky situations if they suddenly strike.

Over To You

By the end of this book, when you've read and inwardly digested all its sound advice and its suggestions for well-thought out hospitality, you will be ready to throw caution to the winds and to set about throwing the best party of your life. So go on, it's up to you now. It's your turn. Take a deep breath, pluck up the courage and just get on with it. Above all, relax and don't worry about a thing – it'll turn out fine, just as you hoped, and with a bit of luck you might even enjoy yourself, too.

Initial Planning

So you've decided to throw a party. You owe so many people invitations, you've been meaning to do it for absolutely ages and you would like the opportunity of using that new dinner service that your mother gave you for Christmas.

But deciding to give a party is only the first step: there are many other things that need to be considered. What kind of event – and on what sort of scale – do you have in mind? The choice is limited only by the size of your home, your budget and your imagination.

A party is a chance for people to gather together. It may be large or small, it may be glamorous or low-key, it may be smart or casual, it may be extravagant or simple and it may be expensive or on a small budget. The guests may be family, friends or colleagues, or they may even be people who don't know each other at all. No matter: given the right atmosphere and a good mix of food and wine, they should be able to conduct a stimulating conversation and, above all, to have a good time.

What Kind of Event?

This is the first decision that you must make right at the start, and there are many different kinds of party to choose from. So think about what you'd like to do, which means asking yourself a lot of questions, such as how many people you want to entertain, how much money you want to spend, what time of day you have in mind, and how much time you've got at your disposal both for preparation and for actually entertaining.

You might, for example, have an intimate supper in mind for a few special close friends, or you might be looking forward to a romantic dinner with a very special friend, or you might prefer to have a simple drinks and nibbles party for all your neighbours, or maybe you'd like a more formal cocktail and finger food party to celebrate a promotion at work. Perhaps your preferred option is a big weekend family lunch with all the children, or an elaborate dinner party with several courses, designed to impress your most important business contacts, or, if

you're really pushing the boat out, you may like to invite a large crowd to a buffet party, which will provide you with the opportunity to entertain more guests than you can conveniently invite to dinner.

Is this to be a really special, once-in-a-lifetime occasion, to celebrate a wedding or christening, perhaps? Or maybe you have no particular reason to celebrate and you simply want to get together with a few friends and nibble on some simple snacks and quaff a few glasses of wine.

Things have changed now and entertaining no longer necessarily means a stuffy, formal three-course meal, eaten on the best china, with beautifully folded napkins. You may prefer to perch on stools around the kitchen table. There are no rules. It's entirely up to you. Because, when all's said and done, this is your party and you must do what suits you.

It's as well to make firm decisions such as these right at the start and to be absolutely sure in your mind exactly what kind of party you're going to give. Impromptu parties sound like a nice idea – if you're lucky, they can be sparky, spontaneous and a great deal of fun – but in fact, they rarely work in practice. Any party is a special event and, as such, it requires a good deal of time and effort.

A Special Occasion

You may want to organize a party in order to mark a special occasion. There are many of these beanfeasts which crop up at regular intervals throughout the year – the main ones being Christmas, New Year and Easter. For many people Christmas is the biggest festivity of the year, bringing with it a grand reunion of the whole family for all those wonderful meals – Christmas Eve supper, Christmas Day lunch, and then all the days afterwards when the challenge is to find as many ways as possible of making delicious meals out of leftover turkey. On the Continent, New Year's Day is often celebrated more than Christmas, with a big family feast either at lunch time or in the evening, depending on what suits the family better. People do not

celebrate Easter nearly as much as Christmas, though old traditions such as Simnel cake and Easter egg hunts crop up in many households throughout the country.

Easter marks the end of the year's annual festivals for most people, though if you are looking for other excuses to have a party, you don't have to look far. There's also St David's Day for the Welsh, St Patrick's Day for the Irish, St Andrew's Day for the Scots, and St George's Day for the English, all of which can be fun to celebrate. But any excuse will do, such as the summer and winter solstices, the first day of spring, midsummer's day, not to mention the host of anniversaries and birthdays of all the members of your family and friends.

Most people don't really need an excuse to have a party, though it can be nice to have a justification – a convenient peg on which to hang an event. In the end, though, when all is said and done, all parties are special occasions. And that's a good enough reason for a celebration. You don't actually need any other reason than that . . .

Planning Ahead

A good party should also be a memorable event, and that needs careful thought. It may sound terribly boring, but the secret of success is careful, forward planning. It is this that ensures that a party goes with a seemingly effortless swing, without the slightest hint of any last-minute panic, from the first germ of an idea to the last crumb under the table.

A good party is one that goes to plan. It isn't usually a matter of luck. It might be, if you're really fortunate, but it's rare and you can't bank on it. The bywords of good party-giving are planning, double-checking and extra double-checking. Don't leave anything to chance and don't take anything for granted.

Most of us have had the misfortune to go to a party that was a dismal failure. Some of us have had the even greater misfortune to give one. But just ask yourself what went wrong, and you'll probably come to the inevitable conclusion that the problem was that the hosts had not thought

through the event with enough care. This may have been because they were inexperienced in the subtle art of entertaining, or it may have been because they had misunderstood their role and obligations as hosts. But the hosts' task is a difficult one. It is much more than a question of hanging up the guests' coats and providing the food and drink. It's a question, too, of giving people a good time, which means making a priority of their comfort and happiness.

Everyone who's ever been to a party – and who hasn't? – knows that the good host or hostess is a relaxed one. It is only against a background of meticulous forethought and organization that you will be able to feel sufficiently at ease to enjoy the party yourself as much as your guests. The good host is in control at all times, but in a subtle and unobtrusive way. He should therefore be skilled in leading and directing conversations, and heading off any potential conflicts that may arise between guests.

The Neighbours

If you've ever lived next door to someone who had the irritating habit of unexpectedly throwing wild parties, with lots of noise and strangers parking their cars all along your street, you'll know just how maddening this can be. But if people are warned beforehand with a polite note, telling them what to expect and until what time, they'll feel differently. So, warn your neighbours in advance, and tell them you hope they won't be too badly disturbed. That way, you'll cut down on the complaints. You might even decide to invite them, too, particularly if it's a large buffet party where one or two extra guests will not be a problem.

Making Lists

As always, planning means making lists. Lots of them: lists of the people you'd like to invite (and any foods they don't eat, whether because of allergy, religion or simple dislike), lists of the wine (and any other drinks) you need to order, lists of the foods you want to serve, lists of your budget, lists of the dishes, cutlery and glasses you need to borrow from a friendly neighbour or hire from a domestic hire company, lists of things you can prepare beforehand and lists of tasks that have to be left until the day, lists of any special things you need to do to get ready for the party and, of course, endless shopping lists – the things you need to order in advance, the things you can buy now and store for later, and the fresh foods you need to buy on the day itself (or on the day before, at the earliest).

A detailed plan may involve several pages and may, as a result, seem like a major headache at the time, but it is well worth making. Some of the most surprising people are inveterate list makers, and they can speak at length about the many advantages of lists: they help you organize your thoughts and get your priorities straight; they act as a schedule of all the tasks that need to be done and therefore make the actual doing of them much more straightforward; and they prevent you forgetting anything important. So take the bull by the horns and make your list of the lists you need to make – you'll be very glad that you did.

LEFT • List-making is the secret of successful party planning. It helps to clarify your thoughts, as well as reminding you to buy, hire or borrow everything that you need.

RIGHT • Glasses, ashtrays, table napkins, cocktail sticks, cocktail stirrers – among the many things you must bear in mind when making your lists.

BELOW RIGHT • A colour theme is an idea worth considering when planning your party. Matching or coordinated candles, napkins and decorations add a certain chic.

Sorting Out the Details

Once you've decided what sort of party you want to give, this provides you with no more than a basic framework. There are still several important decisions that you must make, such as how many guests you want to invite, what time of day and what venue to choose, and, of course, what food and drinks you are going to serve to your guests.

The detail with which you need to plan a party depends, to a large extent, on how big it is. As a general guide, the larger the party, the greater the amount of planning involved. A really large party needs to be planned with almost military precision, if only because if things were to go wrong this could be a large-scale disaster, whereas a smaller get-together obviously doesn't have the same potential for things to go wrong and can therefore be handled in a much more relaxed way.

How Many Guests?

The type of party you decide to give will dictate the number of guests you can comfortably accommodate. For a dinner party, for example, eight people is about the maximum number that most hosts or hostesses can usually contemplate, though six or ten people are also acceptable numbers, depending on the size of the dining table. For a drinks party, 20 is about right, and for a buffet party, 30 is usually the maximum number of people, depending again on the amount of space available.

You don't need to provide seating for a drinks party – just a few chairs dotted about here and there are all that you need to relieve those who can't wait to take the weight off their feet. But if you are going to serve food, people do like to perch somewhere, even if it's just on the arm of a chair or on a cushion on the floor.

What Time of Day?

The time of day you choose to entertain obviously depends on a number of factors, the most important one being how much time you have available and who you want to invite. Perhaps you have no spare time other than Sunday morning, say. Or, if children or elderly people are coming, for example, a lunchtime event would obviously be appropriate, whereas young adults are happy to stay up till all hours and would probably prefer an evening 'do'.

You also need to consider your own staying power and whether you would prefer an early start and a correspondingly early finish, rather than the possibility of having to stay up beyond your preferred bedtime to say your farewells to late revellers. And think, too, about your lifestyle and your own personality, which may, in the end, be the deciding factors. If you are a habitual early riser, for example, it might be better to hold a Sunday brunch party, with a jug of Buck's Fizz and mountains of kedgeree or scrambled egg with smoked salmon and a basket of hot muffins, or a mid-morning coffee party, with coffee and a selection of Danish pastries, cakes and biscuits. There's absolutely no point in

forcing yourself to stay up till the early hours if you've been up since the crack of dawn and you're going to be dead on your feet and longing for your bed before everyone's even arrived – let alone left.

The time of day you choose for your party may also depend on the time of year. Long summer days may suggest one type of event, with long, sparkling, colourful drinks and healthy, all-in-one salads, whereas cosy winter evenings invite quite another, with mulled wine and hot, consoling and sustaining food.

Choosing the Venue

Whether you hold your party at your own home or somewhere else, as well as the number of people you can invite, depends mostly on whether your home is big enough, and on the size of the individual rooms. It is surprising how many people you can fit into quite a small space – as long as they're happy, well fed and in good company (especially if they already know one another), they probably won't really mind being squashed. On the whole, people enjoy being in the centre of a busy throng, and don't object to the occasional traffic jam as long as they're having a good time.

So don't worry too much about overcrowding – an empty, cavernous room in which too few people seem to have turned up is considerably worse and unlikely to achieve anything approaching a party atmosphere. When you are planning a drinks party, measure your rooms and allow about 1.4 square metres/1½ square feet of floor space per person. This is only an approximate calculation, but it generally works as a rough rule of thumb.

Remove ornaments from any level surfaces around the room, such as occasional tables, shelves and sideboards and make sure that these are clear so that people can put down their plates or glasses as they move about.

There are a number of things you can do, too, to maximize the space available. You may need to be inventive and move out large pieces of furniture. If you can serve the food and drinks from the kitchen, for example, and reserve the

dining room for sitting and eating, you may well be able to increase the number of guests for whom you can comfortably cater. Or perhaps you can use the hallway as your bar. And if the weather is fine, you may also be able to spill out into the garden or roof terrace, or you may be able to extend your house with a canopy tacked on to the patio.

If you get on particularly well with your neighbours (and you invite them, too, of course), you may even be able to spill out into the street. In fact, holding a street party – especially if you live in a small street – and sharing the cost with your neighbours can be an excellent way of entertaining, though you will always be at mercy of the weather. Perhaps you might be able to agree some arrangement with your neighbours whereby if it rains you can all retreat indoors, in which case your guests would have a choice of houses and of the different company in them.

Hiring a Venue

If you simply don't have the room and you really want to entertain more people than you can comfortably accommodate in your home, the answer may be to hire a place. You must act fast as many venues get booked up months in advance. Your best bet may be the function room in a local pub, restaurant, hotel or club, but there are many other possibilities, including village halls and club houses. There are yet other ideas, too, which offer much more unusual settings and are perhaps more fun. Throw a party, for example, at your local zoo, or in the Cabinet War Rooms, or in Pinewood Studios, or in the London Dungeon, though there is absolutely no guarantee in this particular venue against the strangest gatecrashers so you'd better beware! Look for venues in the telephone directory, in your local papers, or consult a specialist catering service, some of which pride themselves on offering parties in unusual locations.

Prices vary considerably and some of these locations can cost a lot of money, so what you choose to do will probably depend, to a large extent, on your budget. But there are also other considerations. Some venues, for example, will allow you to use your favourite caterer and to do more or less as you like. Others, however, have strict rules and regulations, and may not allow smoking or even dancing. Yet others may require you to use one of their approved caterers, or even insist that any entertainer or florist be chosen from their approved list. All this, in turn, could bring its own set of restrictions, and this may also affect your choice, as may all the relevant cost implications and any knock-on effect they may have.

Check, too, that your preferred venue has everything you need in terms of kitchen, bathroom and rubbish facilities. If it doesn't, you may have to dig deep into your resources to find alternative and acceptable solutions.

Al Fresco Eating

There is a special magic about eating out of doors under the open sky, and good summer weather really demands an al fresco setting, if at all possible. This need not necessarily mean a vast luxurious garden, nice as this would be. A small garden can be a charming setting, and even a balcony, roof terrace or patio can also make a delightful venue. Picture, for example, an intimate candlelit dinner for two, or four of your nearest and dearest on a sunlit balcony, a strawberries and champagne party with all your closest friends on the patio, or a family barbecue in the back garden. Good weather, good company and good food make a marvellous combination.

Outdoor meals require a different approach to table setting and dressing than meals indoors. Use brightly coloured table linen to show up in strong sunlight and choose dramatic fabrics that you wouldn't dare use indoors, such as net,

RIGHT • Garden benches can double as tables when you are serving food out of doors.

FAR RIGHT • Use lots of cushions to ensure that your garden seating is comfortable, particularly if older people are present.

organza or silk. Take a more relaxed approach to coordinating and matching all the china, glasses and cutlery: a mismatched collection can look highly effective in informal surroundings. Be more extravagant with the flowers to create a romantic setting. Consider decorating the table with huge vases or tiny posies of wild flowers, or sprinkle the cloth with delicate rose petals or violets just for the occasion. Make napkin rings out of twisted trails of ivy or clematis to complete the effect. If it is an evening party, use candles on the tables and lanterns in the trees to create a softly gentle glow after dark.

If you don't have your own garden, you might be able to take a picnic to a local park, or a neighbouring wood, or perhaps to the beach if you live nearby. Just spread plastic sheeting under the rugs or cushions, or take fold-up chairs for the less agile guests, and make any place you fancy your picnic site for the day, with some portable food and a picnic basket. Remember the countryside code, though, and always be careful to take large plastic rubbish bags with you, so that you can take home all your litter and make sure you don't leave any trace of your festivities behind.

Barbecues are always a popular choice, and now that there are small portable barbecues on the market, these can easily be packed in the car and taken to your chosen spot when the fancy takes you – and the weather allows.

Whatever kind of al fresco party you are planning, it's always a good idea to make a contingency plan to fall back on at a moment's notice in case the heavens open and it pours with rain unexpectedly, in which case the whole event risks being a wash-out. You can never be absolutely sure in this country that the weather won't let you down, so make plans accordingly.

RIGHT • *Don't forget to wash and polish all the glasses you'll be using the day before your party – especially those you don't use very often.*

Planning the Refreshments

When you are trying to decide what food to serve your guests, you will need to take into account how much time you are likely to have to spare for cooking. Don't overreach yourself by giving yourself more to do than you have time for, and don't choose a party as the time to practise a dish that you've never attempted before. It isn't: in fact, it would be the worst possible time – you won't know how long it will take to make, let alone what it will taste or even look like.

Even simple foods can be surprisingly time-consuming to prepare and it is important, at this stage, to be realistic and not to allow yourself to be carried away with grand, outrageous ideas that are just not feasible. For this reason, it is a good idea to check in advance that your proposed menu is really workable. Make a rough plan – either in your head or, even better still, on paper – of how long it is going to take you to cook or prepare all the dishes that you've got in mind, and when you're going to be able to fit this into your busy schedule.

Don't forget, too, to allow enough time for all those irritating extra little jobs that all too often slip the memory and are left until the last minute, when they send you into a blind panic. Remember, for example, to allow a reasonable amount of time for setting and decorating the table, any last-minute emergency housework you need to do before the event, arranging flowers if you're planning to have them, making ice and chilling drinks, washing any glasses or plates that haven't been used for a long time, rearranging the furniture, and so on.

It's a good idea, too, to consider how much time you would need, according to your proposed menu, to spend away from your guests attending to all those 'little' jobs that actually take so long, such as stirring, whisking, arranging and garnishing food. You must not forget this time factor. You may be the only person present who knows all the guests, and your presence may therefore be essential in order to introduce people to one another, to bring reluctant guests into the conversation, to guide the conversation towards subjects that you know to be of mutual interest, and thus to make the party go with a swing.

Theme Parties

If you're stuck for ideas, a theme party may be the answer. It's not only fun but it can also give you a framework within which to plan all those important details, such as the table decorations and even the food.

A French Bistro party, for example, is more interesting than just an ordinary buffet supper, while Vicars and Tarts is a traditional favourite theme. Another possibility is to choose the Seven Deadly Sins as your theme and to ask your guests to come symbolic of a particular sin. This is bound to get them thinking and to cause a lot of laughter.

Children are particularly keen on themed parties, and there's nothing they enjoy more than dressing up as pirates, witches or fairies. The guests (or their parents!) can make the costumes themselves, or they can be hired from specialist party or costume shops, which have grown up in every town centre and provide a somewhat more expensive but much simpler solution.

A popular option for a children's party is hiring an entertainer – a juggler or magician, for example – and there is no reason why there should not be an adult equivalent at an adult party. Suggestions include a live band, which can be a wonderful choice, especially in an al fresco setting, or perhaps a string quartet for a sedate tea or drinks party in the late afternoon or early evening.

RIGHT • Masks are as far as some people can be persuaded to venture in terms of fancy dress, but they can be great fun.

FAR RIGHT • For an al fresco party, don't forget to provide lighting for the garden, with lanterns, hurricane lamps or fairy lights.

Invitations

Making the Guest List

Having decided what sort of event you are going to host, the guest list is probably one of the first – and also the most important – lists that you are likely to make. You may not think that this is necessary, especially if you are planning only a small dinner party for, say, eight people. But a guest list is more than just a list of the people you are inviting: it is also the first step in your planning, a working document, and you check the names on it for numbers, balance (men to women, age, etc, though it's no longer essential to make sure that you always invite exactly equal numbers of men and women and a lot of people are more relaxed about this now) and, of course, compatibility. There may, for example, be people on your list, when you see it in black and white on the page in front of you, who you just know don't get on terribly well, and you will then have to consider whether it would be better not to invite them together, or whether there will be enough other people there to dilute their differences sufficiently for them not to matter too much.

Try to invite people who have shared interests. Avoid inviting too many people who have exactly the same professions or people whose lifestyles are too similar, or your party may soon turn into a miniature convention for computer buffs, or a tactical planning meeting for people who play golf, or bridge, or whatever. Too tight a common bond between people can all too soon turn into a bind for everyone else in the room!

Don't get carried away and invite more people than you had originally intended to. Remember how carefully you'd thought about numbers when you made your list. There was a sensible reason for that, so stick to it, otherwise you may find that you've invited more people than you can comfortably accommodate and you will be hit by the nasty feeling that you might not be able to cope.

Make up a 'reserves' list, too. Then, if anyone has to turn your invitation down, you don't need to panic and you can easily make up the numbers from your list of reserves.

A guest list also acts as a simple reminder to invite everyone on it. That sounds obvious and you may not think that you need to be reminded, but the memory can, on occasion, be a treacherous participant in such matters. People are increasingly busy nowadays, and it is surprising how something as obvious and simple as this can sometimes be forgotten in a busy schedule when you've already got a host of other things on your mind.

A guest list obviously takes on greater and greater importance as the numbers involved in your proposed social event get bigger. The larger the party, the more complicated it gets, the more difficult it is to be sure that the numbers are right and that you've achieved the right balance, and the harder it will be to keep track of replies.

If you are giving a drinks or buffet party, for example, you can probably reckon on about one in six of the people you invite either turning your invitation down or not turning up on the day. It is a good idea, therefore, to allow for this by inviting more people to start with – say, 25 rather than 20, 35 rather than 30, 60 rather than 50. This is a much safer principle on which to work than suddenly trying to come up with suitable substitutes at the last minute.

The Invitations

Issuing invitations is perhaps one of the most pleasurable parts of giving a party. It's all fun and no hard work (yet!), and it gets people in the mood. Contacting friends is always fun and this is a joyous reason to get in touch, and people enjoy receiving invitations so this is an agreeable social interchange, encouraging as it does pleasant feelings of sociability and anticipation.

Whether the party is formal or informal, and whether you are telephoning or sending handwritten invitations or gold-embossed ones with fancy engraving, the one thing that is certain is that people definitely all need some kind of proper invitation. Otherwise, they won't know where to go and when.

People tend to be a lot less formal than they used to be, and many prefer to invite their friends in person or on the telephone, rather than by written invitation. There are really no hard-and-fast rules, and there are pros and cons to both procedures. So the choice is really up to you. You're the boss, and that starts with the invitations.

By Telephone

Telephoning is often a good way of transmitting an invitation, particularly if you know the people well. It's not only a rapid way of

communicating with them, but it's also the quickest and most efficient way of extracting an early, if not immediate, reply.

Similarly, any face-to-face invitation is perfectly acceptable, too, whether it's transmitted in the pub, on the tube, in the office, at the door, in the swimming pool, or at the school gates. It's all too easy, however, in any face-to-face situation, to forget to pass on all those important details – perhaps because you're in a hurry, or excited, or you've got other things on your mind, or worried about what you're going to have for supper, or you're just terribly busy.

The most important things that you need to say are:

- the date
- the time
- what kind of party it is (i.e. drinks or dinner, or whatever – there's nothing worse than

bolting down supper before you go out only to be served great food which you can't manage!

- the address
- what to wear
- how to get there

A lot of people also like to ask their host how many other people will be there, and perhaps even who they are likely to be.

So if you choose to communicate with your friends in this way, plan what you're going to say in advance – perhaps written on a piece of paper as a checklist of all the relevant details – and be sure not to leave anything out.

In Writing

There are certain advantages to sending a written invitation, the most obvious one being, quite simply, that people like to receive a written card. This may sound trivial, but it is an important part of the social interchange between people. It makes them feel they are receiving special treatment and that the party is therefore all the more special an occasion. An invitation, which can be as smart or as informal as you feel is appropriate to the occasion in question, gets the party off to a flying start from the word go. In addition, those people who receive a card will probably put it on a shelf or on the mantelpiece, where it will then serve as a useful reminder.

With a written invitation, you can be quite sure you remember to give all the salient details and you don't leave anything out. Invitees need to know precisely what it is they are being invited to and exactly what they are expected to do in terms of place, time etc.

Again, above all, they need to know the following details:
- the date
- the time
- what kind of party it is (e.g. drinks or dinner)
- you can also mark the time you'd like them to go home. In the old days, this matter was dealt with discreetly with the useful phrase, 'Carriages, 10pm'. Nowadays, an acceptable way of saying this is, for example, 'Drinks 12.00–1.30pm', or 'Coffee 3.30–5.30pm'. If you don't mind how long people stay, put 'from 8pm', for example, which should get the message across, and if you'd like them to go earlier – perhaps you have elderly neighbours or the noise might disturb the children – say something along the lines of '8 till around midnight'. Most people will understand this and will not be offended by it.
- the address
- any dress requirements, such as Black Tie, Lounge Suits, or Fancy Dress, which it would be quite inexcusable not to point out!
- and how to get there if they don't already know, preferably with a map or at least clear instructions if your home is particularly difficult to find. The best bet is probably to enclose a photocopy of the relevant page in a local A–Z street finder or road map, marking the position of your home with a brightly-coloured highlighter pen.

When to Send Your Invitations

Always send your invitations in plenty of time, so that your friends have ample advance warning. The usual time for a large function – say, a big birthday party or christening – is about six to eight weeks. The time for a wedding is often even longer, because the church or registry office has to be booked in advance. A formal dinner party needs about three or four weeks' warning. And if you want to do something on a day that is special for everyone – say, on Valentine's Day or New Year's Eve, for example – you will probably need to make your plans and tell people even earlier than this.

That doesn't mean, of course, that you will never be able to take advantage of the weather and to make a last-minute decision to hold a barbecue the day before, or to ring your friends and ask them to come round for an impromptu supper. There's nothing wrong with spur-of-the-moment entertaining – it can be very nice – but be careful, because it doesn't always work.

Getting the Details Right

Don't send out your invitations until you are absolutely sure of all the details. There's no point sending out invitations when you haven't yet confirmed the time and place, or you may end up with all round confusion and many irate guests even before the evening has begun.

You must be certain, for example, that you will be able to fulfil all your plans, including your chosen place and time, and that you will be able to do all this within your budget. Don't commit yourself to anything in terms of invitations when your party is still no more than a twinkle in your eye, not a future certainty.

Replies

People don't always bother – or remember – to reply to an invitation when it's sitting quietly minding its own business on their mantelpiece, but there are various ways in which you can

encourage a reply. The traditional method is to put RSVP on your invitation, which encourages people to tell you whether or not they are coming. If you don't hear from them, you can then always telephone and ask people if they are intending to come. If this doesn't prompt them, nothing will. Another system, adopted by many Americans, is to put 'regrets only'. This invites people to reply only if they are not able to come, or 'only with regrets', so if they don't reply you can assume that they are, indeed, coming. The advantage of this system is that it is a lot simpler but the disadvantage, on the other hand, is that, if you don't hear from them, you have to assume they are coming and you might still be wrong. This is therefore a slightly risky procedure and you can hardly then telephone and ask them to tell you without seeming to be either neurotic, stupid or rude.

The most efficient way of being absolutely sure of replies is to send out a reply card with your invitation, so that all people have to do is to fill it out to say whether they are coming or not and pop it in the post. And if you're not worried that your guests might think it patronising, you could even stick a stamp on to it so they don't even have to go to the Post Office to buy stamps.

No method is foolproof, but replies are important because they enable the hosts to keep track of how many people they can expect. It is therefore important, too, to keep a record of your replies, especially acceptances, together with any special dietary needs which you may not have known about before. This is another way in which your guest list can come in useful, providing you with a simple way of doing this, simply add a cross or tick to the list, together with any additional information that you need to remember.

As with anything to do with entertaining, it's best to remember that you trust to your memory at your peril. Who hasn't wondered, as they lay the table for dinner – did he say he was definitely coming, come what may, or that he would only be able to come if his wife had recovered from the flu? This is where your list will come into its own putting at bay any such last minute worries.

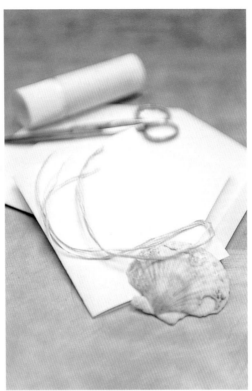

> *Mr and Mrs Jo Public*
>
> *request the pleasure of your company*
> *on the engagement of their daughter*
>
> *Jane to ...*

> *John Smith and Helen Evans*
>
> *would like you to come to a party*
> *to celebrate their engagement*

The Wording

How to word your invitations is not written in stone. True, there are accepted traditional ways of doing this, some of which are shown above. But if you want to break with tradition and to design your own cards, which may be as festive and colourful – even brash – as you like, that's perfectly acceptable, too.

Making Your Own Invitations

If you do not want the added expense of printed invitations, it is quite acceptable to make your own. These can be done in any style or format you choose. They can be hand written, drawn or printed on your home computer, and posted or faxed to your guests, or perhaps delivered by hand and popped through the relevant front door.

Making your own invitations gives you an opportunity to stamp your own personality on the occasion right from the start

RIGHT • Introduce the theme of your party from the start with the invitation. For a sea world dinner party, punch some holes in your invite and secure a pretty sea shell to the front of the card with some raffia.

ABOVE and RIGHT • For your midsummer tea party, make some pretty invitations, using pieces of bold floral wallpaper stuck to a piece of card. Use a hole punch and add some pink ribbon tied in a bow.

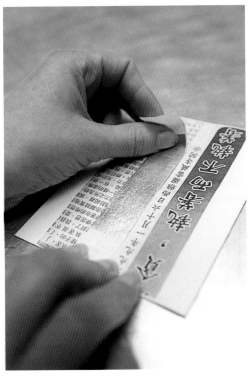

ABOVE and RIGHT • An Oriental buffet party requires an Oriental treatment for the invitations, too. Use some sheets of Chinese newspaper and Chinese incense paper to evoke a truly Eastern atmosphere.

ABOVE and RIGHT • For a Mexican dinner party, make a colourful invitation by sticking a piece of plastic-coated fabric to some coloured card. It is easy to make an envelope by using an existing envelope as a template.

ABOVE and RIGHT • A cocktail party invitation requires stylish treatment. Stick half a cocktail umbrella to some black card. Make an envelope by using an existing envelope as a template, and line it with tissue paper.

Setting the Scene

Parties are all about celebration, which is why it's so important to set the scene. This immediately gives everyone the message 'party' and makes sure that everyone's in the right festive mood from the start.

The trick, though, is to do it without it being obvious to your guests. It must appear natural, seamless, easy, effortless – and not something that's taken you hours – days, even – of hard work behind the scenes in preparation for that glorious moment that you've been preparing yourself for all along, when you open the door with a winning smile on your face, looking as though you don't have a care in the world.

Creating the Atmosphere

There are a myriad ways of creating just the right party atmosphere. These don't need to be complicated or expensive – it may be surprising but sometimes it's the simplest things that say party the loudest.

Light the candles, put the mulled wine on the stove and sit back: tempting aromas, a touch of glitter and oodles of goodwill are all you need to inject a little party thrill into the air. Deck out your surroundings in the brightest of colours and the gaudiest of decorations, and put the table in its glad rags. This is not the time for discretion – it's the time, rather, for all things loud, vulgar and, above all, fun ...

Getting your Home Ready

If possible, get started the day before the party. It's a particularly good idea, for example, to make sure the house is ready in advance. That includes all those seemingly little things that actually take surprisingly longer than you expect, like moving the furniture, cleaning and arranging the flowers.

Your home needs to make a welcoming statement to your guests from the moment they walk through the front door. It's all very well making sure that the room where the party is being held looks sparkling and festive, but if the first thing that people see as they arrive is a

mess, that will hardly make the right kind of impression and make them feel at home.

So the first thing you need to do is to make the hall – or entrance lobby or cloakroom, or whatever you have in your home as you arrive – look warm and friendly.

Above all, it goes without saying that it should be clean and tidy. How you then add welcoming, festive touches is entirely up to you. These can be as simple or as elaborate as you like. You might arrange a vase of flowers on the hall table, for example, or you might put a coloured bulb in the lampshade, or you might even decorate the hall with balloons or streamers. It all depends on the type of party and the sort of atmosphere you have decided to create for the event.

ABOVE and RIGHT • For a party on a Mexican theme, decorate your table using patterned plastic-covered fabric, plastic flowers, brightly-coloured serviettes and plates. Drape the walls with a Mexican throw. Candles and little pots of cacti are good finishing touches.

Think, too, in advance about where people are going to put their coats. This may be in a cupboard in the hall, in which case you will need to make sure there is enough room in it. Or it may be on a bed in someone's bedroom or in the spare room, in which case you will have to make sure that this room is tidy as people will be going in there as well.

And then there are all those little things that can so easily be forgotten but which can save you time on the day if you think of them in advance. Make sure, for example, that there are enough hand towels for the bathroom (or bathrooms if you'll be using more than one). Get a first aid kit ready in case of emergencies – they don't often happen, but they do happen.

Make a note of the local taxi service and pin this up near the telephone, in case you find yourself inundated by requests for this at going home time, when you're bound to have rather more important things to do, like saying a proper goodbye to your guests and telling them how nice it has been to see them and you hope you'll see them soon, and so on.

Have a roll of kitchen paper and a dustpan and brush within easy reach for dealing with all those little spills that are almost bound to happen at least once in the evening! Have ready a bottle of soda water or a bottle of white wine, either of which will neutralize red wine stains and make them easier to remove later, when everyone's gone home.

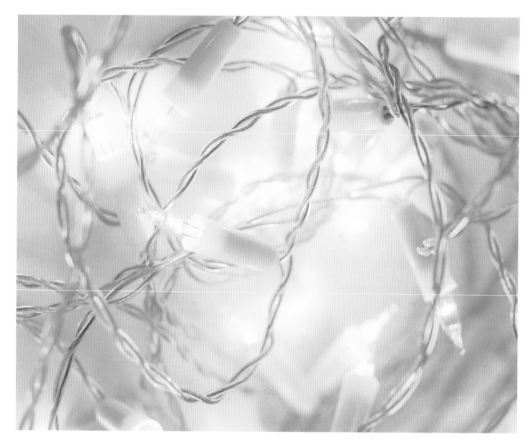

Arranging the Furniture

Just how much furniture you want in the room when you're entertaining depends, to a large extent, on what sort of party you are throwing. You will therefore need to give some practical thought to this before people arrive, in terms of how many people are coming and what they'll be doing most of the time (i.e. sitting or standing).

If you're having a dinner party, for instance, people will spend most of their time sitting down. Far from clearing a space and removing furniture, you'll need to make sure that there are enough chairs for everyone – both for drinks before dinner and then for sitting round the table and eating. So work out your requirements beforehand. If you don't possess enough chairs, you can always borrow some from friends or neighbours but be sure to do this before the event. Above all, don't wait until people arrive before you suddenly realise that you don't have enough chairs and you have to rush off next

door to see what you can beg, borrow or steal. This can be embarrassing, so always be prepared. Whether you sit at a round or oblong table obviously depends on what you have, so you're unlikely to be making that choice just before dinner. If you do have a choice, though, it's worth bearing in mind that a round table is probably a more sociable setting – it draws everyone into the conversation rather than encouraging people to split off into little groups, as often happens at an oblong table, where people tend to talk just their immediate neighbours and to ignore everyone else.

If you're giving a drinks or cocktail party, on the other hand, things will be very different. In this case, people will probably be standing most of the time and you won't need chairs except, perhaps, for two or three dotted about for the more weary members of the party who need to take the weight off their feet from time to time. Nothing gets in the way of this sort of party more than a lot of large cumbersome pieces of unwanted furniture, which are quite obviously superfluous to requirements and get in people's

RIGHT • Decorating the room for an Oriental buffet party is surprisingly easy, using Chinese banners and decorations that can be found relatively cheaply in Oriental supermarkets. Add to the decoration by encouraging guests to come wearing silk pyjamas, kimonos and chopsticks in their hair.

way, preventing them from circulating freely. You will therefore have to clear away as much furniture as possible to make space for people not only to stand but also to move about and mingle among the other guests without tripping themselves up.

Decorating the Room

Whether and how you decorate the room will depend on what sort of party you're having, the occasion and the mood you want to create. But whatever you do, it is somehow important to

LEFT • To create a really summery feel for an outdoor, midsummer tea party, the chairs can be beautifully decorated for the occasion by draping a piece of chiffon material over their backs. A bow and a fresh rose add just the right finishing touch.

someone's birthday, you might like to decorate the room accordingly, with streamers, balloons or whatever you feel is most appropriate to the particular festive occasion and the person involved. Some people don't like a fuss and it is worth bearing this in mind, too, and keeping things simple.

Lighting

The lighting always plays an important part in setting the mood of a room, so make sure you choose carefully. Several lamps set around the room are probably best – including shaded table lamps and uplighters – and are certainly much more atmospheric than one central ceiling light, which can be stark and rather austere. The resulting light should not be too bright but should bathe the room in a warm, twinkling glow. If you're feeling ambitious, you might even want to change the lighting over the course of the evening. You may like to start with a fairly bright light, clear enough for people to see what they are eating, and then dim the lights so that later on – over coffee or dancing, perhaps – it is subdued.

Remember, too, what they say about candlelight – that it hides a multitude of sins. It's true and it can make even the drabbest, most unattractive room look wonderful, bringing it to life and lending it a dramatic, almost magical quality. Make sure that any candles are put somewhere safe, where they are not likely to set fire to fabric or flowers. Don't put them on the floor, where they can easily be kicked over or set fire to people's long skirts and trouser legs. If you intend to light up your garden using Chinese paper lanterns, be careful if you are using candles, as these should be properly secured and checked on a regular basis.

make the room feel special. It goes without saying that this is a special event and the room should reflect that.

If you're having a simple drinks party, you are unlikely to want to decorate the room much, though a few flower arrangements always look attractive. These can be as simple or as dramatic as you like, depending on the flowers and time you have at your disposal, your personal taste and how good you are at flower arranging.

Always make sure that any flowers you use are in the best condition, preferably buying or picking them that morning or the day before. Highly scented flowers can be gorgeous but a strong perfume can be overpowering, particularly when people are eating and it competes with the delicious aroma of the food.

If you're hosting a party at Christmas, you'll probably want to have your Christmas tree and decorations up. Similarly, if you're celebrating

Combining candles with flowers can make for an attractive arrangement, while also being a good thing to do for its space-saving qualities. Either insert a candle into a piece of florists' foam on a saucer and arrange the flowers around it, or use a specially-designed foam ring that sits on a candlestick around a narrow candle. Don't forget, though, that flowers are also flammable and be wary of any danger before it has the chance to strike.

ABOVE • It is often the details that are crucial in setting the scene. Simple white candles look great in stylish candlesticks, while well-chosen white table linen and crockery create a beautifully-laid table.

ABOVE, RIGHT and BELOW • To create your own candles for a sea world party, melt some wax in a heatproof jug over hot water. Place a wick in an oyster shell, dipping it in wax first to secure it to the shell. Pour in the melted wax in layers, allow each layer to harden before adding another layer, and continue until the shell is full.

Laying the Dining Table

Give some thought in advance to whether you have enough plates, dishes, glasses and cutlery for your special party. If you don't, you may be able to borrow some from friends or neighbours, or perhaps you can hire glasses from your local off-licence which is supplying the wine. There are several companies that hire out all sorts of things that can come in useful for just such an occasion, including china, glassware, tablecloths and even kitchen equipment. Find out what their terms are and, if it doesn't cost any extra, try to get possession the day before, which should give you plenty of time to unpack and check it all. Some hire firms will even allow you to return all the things you borrowed dirty – which will probably cost you extra but will be worth it in terms of the considerable time and effort that it will save you.

The way in which you set your table is as much a reflection of your tastes and personality as is the food that you serve. Some people are much more relaxed about what they use and how they arrange it than others, but when you're throwing a really special party and you want to impress, always use the best that you possess. It may mean visiting the attic to dig out seldom-used china and washing it painstakingly before the day, but when you see how beautiful your table is, you will agree that it was worth it.

Entertaining is a good excuse for showing off your most treasured china, cutlery, glasses and table linen, and it is the first impression that your guests will receive of the culinary pleasures to come. Remember, too, that the overall style of the table should be in keeping with the occasion. For example, a damask cloth and shining silver would be out of place for an informal supper, while a brightly coloured checked cloth would probably be inappropriate for a formal dinner with business colleagues. But whatever you are doing and however formal or informal the occasion, make sure you take the effort to make sure the table looks just right, and pay attention to every last detail.

It may sound obvious, but a lot of people forget how important the look of the dining table is. You and your guests will be looking at it for the best part of the evening, and it is this which, above all else, sets the scene for the party. So, with this in mind, aim for a beautifully laid table, covered in a rich glow of glinting glasses and shiny cutlery.

An eye-catching centrepiece is always attractive, too. This might be something colourful and edible, such as a bowl of fruit or gourds. And then, of course, there are flowers. If you have a flower arrangement in the centre of the table, make sure that it isn't too tall for people to see each other over the top. The flowers should fit in with the general colour scheme of the table setting, perhaps picking out the colours of the napkins or the crockery. Each flower should be as near perfect as possible, because they will be viewed so close-up.

ABOVE • Arrange flowers to make an eye-catching centrepiece for your table, being careful to coordinate the colours with your table linen and crockery.

RIGHT • Make sure that you coordinate your crockery and table linen in advance for your midsummer tea party. A variety of different floral fabrics may be used, thereby creating an eclectic mix of styles and colours.

Remember, too, that the arrangement should be equally pretty from all sides, as people will be sitting all round it. If you are in any doubt and you have a cake-decorating turntable, it's a good idea to put your arrangement on that as you create it and turn it around to view it from all angles, just as your guests will be seeing it.

Be creative with your containers. A hollowed-out orange or a Savoy cabbage makes a fitting and attractive receptacle for a few well-chosen stems. Make holes in the cabbage with a sharp skewer and insert the flower stems into the holes at the last minute before the meal.

And if there is no space in the centre of the table, consider making a tiny flower arrangement for each guest as part of their place setting. Even a single flower in a glass or egg cup looks attractive. A few choice flower heads look lovely floating in a bowl of water, especially if you have chosen a particularly beautiful bowl. Add floating candles to your bowl as a finishing touch.

Whether you have a gleaming polished table set with heat-resistant table mats or a beautiful embroidered tablecloth is up to you. If you have a tablelcloth, it is a good idea, before you start to lay the table, to spread a blanket over the table top under the tablecloth. This will not only protect the polished surface of the dining table, but it will also give an added comfortable 'depth' to your tablecloth, as well as dulling the sound of clashing cutlery and crockery, which can be quite overwhelming, particularly if you have invited a lot of guests.

Some people like to write out the menu clearly on coloured card or pretty handmade paper to coordinate with the rest of the table setting, and to put it on the table in front of each place setting. You can arrange the menus in pretty picture frames, or you can just stand the cards directly on the table. This both tells your guests what they are eating and what to expect for the rest of the meal.

Separate tables for children are a good idea if you are entertaining friends with children. The children enjoy the special treatment, and if you seat them around a coffee table, they can sit on cushions on the floor to minimize the chances of spillage and accidents.

The Cutlery

The easiest rule for setting cutlery at each place setting is to position it in the order in which it will be used, working from the outside inwards towards the plate. This goes as follows (this applies, obviously, only to those items of cutlery that you're using):

On the left:	On the right:
First course fork	First course knife
Fish fork	Fish knife
Main course fork	Main course knife
Dessert fork	Dessert spoon

ABOVE • Napkins provide a pleasing finishing touch on a well-laid table, particularly if they have been beautifully folded. Linen napkins obviously look best but, failing that, paper ones are a good substitute.

If you're having soup as your first course, the soup spoon goes where the first course knife is and the first course fork would be absent. Some people prefer to put the dessert spoon and fork across the top of each place setting, the spoon

above the fork with its handle towards the right, and the fork's handle towards the left. If you are using a butter knife, this can go on the far right, though some people prefer to put it under the dessert spoon and fork at the top of the place

setting, and others again like to put it on the side plate. There are various fashions and theories as to their best position but, in the end, it's up to you and it doesn't really matter. Do whatever is most convenient and, above all, you mustn't worry about it, either as a host or a guest.

The Glasses

Set the glasses for white wine, red wine and water in a triangle at the top right of each place setting. An alternative arrangement is to put the glasses in a straight horizontal line, working

in the opposite way from the cutlery. In other words, they are used in order from the plate outwards, starting with a white wine glass, red wine glass and lastly a dessert wine glass to accompany the dessert. A water glass can be placed behind the others.

For an informal dinner, you don't need such a formal table setting. Something simpler will immediately create a comfortable atmosphere and put guests at their ease. Glasses should still be used from the inside out, but it is normal to use fewer glasses at an informal occasion. A glass for wine and another one for water is usually sufficient.

TOP LEFT • If you are catering for a crowd, roll up your napkins and secure with ribbon.

TOP RIGHT • A fresh rose, name tag and some ribbon make an effective table setting.

BOTTOM LEFT • Brightly-coloured napkins and plastic flowers look great for a Mexican party.

BOTTOM RIGHT • Unusual partners, such as raffia and sea shells, make a welcome change.

Napkins

Setting the table is about much more than arranging the cutlery and glasses. There is no easier way of making a table special than by dressing it with a well-chosen tablecloth and napkins, plain or fancy. Napkins are not only practical, they can also be stylish design elements. They offer great scope, from simple paper ones that are available in every conceivable colour, to elegant crisply starched linen ones, plain or embroidered, which are a great sign of luxury and can be imaginatively folded or simply laid on side plates, perhaps in a napkin ring. Napkins won't take up much room on a crowded table, but they will give instant definition to each place setting.

Butter

If you are having a formal dinner party and you feel you need to put some butter on the table for use during the meal, it's probably best to put little cubes, curls or pats in four little dishes for a party of eight people, say, and arrange them about the table. This saves people having to wait for people to pass the butter.

Store shaped butters in a bowl of cold water and ice cubes in the refrigerator covered with clingfilm until you are ready to put the butter out on the table, when you should decorate it with sprigs of parsley. It should be neither too soft nor straight from the refrigerator and too hard. Aim for a spreadable consistency.

Finger Bowls

If you are planning to serve any food that is to be eaten with the fingers – asparagus, globe artichokes or spare ribs, for example – you should place a finger bowl beside each guest's place before you serve it. These may seem old-fashioned, but they are highly practical. Half-fill each glass bowl with tepid water, to which you have added a little lemon juice or rosewater. You may also like to put in a flower head or a slice of lemon, which will float attractively on the top. Remove the finger bowls as soon as they have been used. You can either give extra paper napkins to use while they are eating with their fingers, or offer your guests clean napkins in preparation for the next course.

Seating People

You will probably have given some thought to who will get on with whom when you compiled your original list of the people you wanted to invite. You may have a clear idea in your head of where everyone should sit and, in this case, seating people is unlikely to present too much of a problem.

Even so, you should think about it in advance so that, when it comes to the event, you know exactly where to tell your guests to sit. So often, when everyone crowds round the table questioningly and asks where they should sit, your plan can go clean out of your head and everyone ends up sitting where they want, which is not always the best arrangement. You can put place cards at each place setting, indicating who should sit where. An interesting way of doing this is to make individual place cards in interesting shapes – perhaps stars, trees, bells or whatever you like – with coloured paper or card, a felt-tipped pen and a ribbon, and tie these in front of each place setting. A fun and original idea is to write names on large pebbles or shells, using a gold or black marker, and put these at each place setting. Even if you don't go to these lengths, you should probably make a note of your table plan on a card, if only to remind you.

People are a lot less formal than they used to be and they no longer tend to expect strict man/woman/man/woman arrangements, so seating plans don't need to be as contrived as they once were. Do, however, give some thought to who you are going to seat next to whom.

Try, for example, to avoid seating painfully shy people next to one another, as this can produce a weak link in the conversation around the table. Avoid, too, seating two people next to one another who are particularly loud and always like to be the centre of attention, as they may simply spend all their time competing with each other and feeling sulky and bad-tempered whenever they are outdone.

It is also best, if at all possible, to avoid seating people next to one another who work together, or who are in the same line of business. Otherwise, they may end up talking shop all evening, which could be excruciatingly boring for everyone else at the table. It's generally best, too, to separate couples, or they may simply resume the row that they were having on their way to your party.

ABOVE, RIGHT and BELOW • For a Mexican place setting with a difference, buy a few little pots of cacti and paint them with brightly-coloured enamel paint. Place them on a plate with some multi-coloured confetti.

ABOVE, RIGHT and BELOW • This Mexican place setting is so simple to make but so effective. Write the name of your guest on a coloured luggage tag and attach it to a glass with a brightly coloured plastic clothes peg, then slip in a plastic flower to finish it off.

ABOVE, RIGHT and BELOW • If you are holding a sea world dinner party, why not have some fun creating sand castle place settings? All you need are some cocktail sticks, white card, sand and a mould. Make sure that you do not put the sand castle on to a plate that your guests will be eating off!

ABOVE, RIGHT and BELOW • Fold your napkin neatly to form a rectangular shape and tie a name tag to it with some ribbon in a bow. Add a fresh rosebud for a finishing touch, and place on each guest's plate.

ABOVE, RIGHT and BELOW • For an imaginative Oriental place setting, wrap a fortune cookie in some cellophane, secure this with raffia, and add a tag made from Chinese newspaper and Chinese incense paper. Write each guest's name on the back.

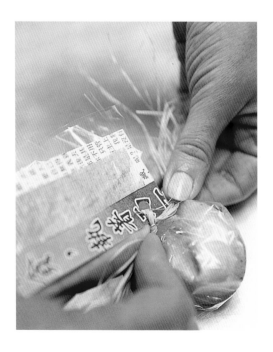

A Buffet Table

The buffet table should present your guests with a really eye-catching display. This will act as a great temptation for their appetites and lure them over to fill their plates.

In addition to this, the food should be easy to manage with a need for the least possible (if any) cutlery. Everything should be within easy reach, and those dishes requiring spoons are best positioned at the front of the table. Taller, pedestal-type dishes can then be put further back on the table. To ease crowding, it is best to present all the peripheral things people need other than the main course – for example, the cheese, cutlery, napkins and desserts – on separate tables or trolleys. Wrapping the cutlery in napkins makes it easier for people to pick them all up together. If you are having a large crowd of people, it is a good idea to repeat some of the foods somewhere else on the table, so that people can approach from both ends rather than all following each other laboriously in the same direction.

If you want to put a flower arrangement on a buffet table, bear in mind that the principles for its design are quite different from those for a dining table. An arrangement on a buffet table needs to be tall enough and dramatic enough to be seen from a distance, and should be important enough to take over as the centre of attention when the dishes of food begin to get empty. If you have a star dish on the table – perhaps a cold poached salmon or a cold turkey, for example – underline its important role as the centre of attention by placing two matching flower arrangements on each side of it.

People like to know exactly what it is that they're eating, so if it's not obvious from the appearance of the dish – as with sandwiches and foods that have been cooked in pastry, for instance – you might like to write the name of each dish on an identification tag and place it alongside the dishes. Alternatively, you could write it on a gift tag and tape it to the dishes, or write it on a triangular 'flag' and attach it with glue to a cocktail stick. This can look very attractive, as well as being a great help for your guests to identify the food.

Getting Help

It's strange to say, but people often recoil from the idea of paying for someone to help them give their party – but why? There's absolutely no shame in admitting that you could do with some help. Don't assume that you have to do everything yourself – because you don't.

If you're planning a large-scale party, you may like to go the whole hog and hire a professional caterer or party planner, who will take the whole thing in hand for you. This has the great advantage of relieving you of both most of the hard work and the headache, leaving you free to talk to your guests and to have fun – which is, after all, what parties are all about.

The best way of selecting a caterer is by personal recommendation, and if you're not already familiar with the sort of food they offer, ask them to give you an advance tasting, so you can relax, confident in the knowledge that your expectations will be met. Check in advance, too, on all the details, which may sound trivial but are in fact so important to the success, or otherwise, of any event. Look at their table linen, china, glasses, and so on, to check that you will like their style of table setting.

If your budget doesn't stretch to a caterer or you would prefer to do the cooking yourself, you may still decide that you could do with some help serving the food. You can hire waiting staff, who don't do the cooking but just the serving, or you can ask a catering college to send a student, or you may be able to enlist willing volunteers among your teenage children or your friends who are prepared to help you. Whoever is helping, make sure that you give everyone specific duties and brief them fully before people arrive, so that they know exactly what you expect them to do. Ask them to arrive about an hour or two in advance, so that they can help you set everything up, learn where everything is and understand exactly what it is they are meant to be doing.

Once you've decided that you do indeed need help, the next question is how much and how many people? Every party set-up is different, but there are certain guidelines that can come in useful. If you're planning a gathering of about 20 to 30 people, serving drinks and finger foods, you will probably need a minimum of three people: a host to welcome guests and look after their coats, someone to pass the food, and someone to look after the drinks. If you're expecting more than 30 people, you will probably need at least four people: a host to welcome guests and look after coats, two to pass the food, and one to serve drinks. Increase the number according to the number of guests on the basis of one person per 15 guests to serve food, and one per 15 guests to serve wine.

Clearing-up

Masochists apart, few people would disagree with the view that clearing-up after a party is absolutely no fun at all. That said, though, there's no getting away from it and it just has to be done.

It's therefore worth thinking about it in advance, which may actually make it easier. There are things, for example, that could save you a lot of trouble at clearing-up time if you do them in advance. There's nothing better, for a start, than spending a little time clearing the decks. Perhaps you could remove all those superfluous things that you won't be needing from your work surfaces, for instance, kitchen appliances, bread bins, plants, cake tins, and so on. Empty the dishwasher and clear a special space, preferably out of sight, where you can pile up all the dirty dishes in neat stacks as you go. Have a large bowl ready nearby, into which you can scrape all the debris on the used plates before stacking them together in a pile. Buy extra rolls of kitchen paper, and wipe any plates which have mayonnaise on them before washing them. If you don't do this, mayonnaise gets in the washing-up water and leaves a fine film of grease on everything. Grade all the china in different sizes when you clear up. Put the glasses together somewhere, not stacked inside each other which can make them difficult to separate, and soak the cutlery in a large bowl of hot soapy water to make washing up much easier when you get around to it.

RIGHT • Don't throw away any Champagne corks. They can be used as good luck charms – simply cut into the base and stick in a silver coin – and give them to your guests as a gift.

There's nothing more irritating than piles of empty bottles, which tend to accumulate just anywhere – on the table, in the hall and on the floor, where they lie just waiting to trip people up. So put a large, empty cardboard box near the bin, ready to receive bottles as and when they become empty.

Ideas for Themed Parties

Themed parties are a lot of fun and have become quite fashionable these days. If the thought of throwing a themed party sends you into an instant panic and you don't quite know where to start, rest assured and relax. There are almost as many ways in which you can arrange a themed party as there are people throwing parties.

They are not actually particularly difficult to organise, because a lot of the hardest work is done by the guests. You'll be surprised, in fact, at how enthusiastic and enterprising people are when it comes to making the effort to dress the part. The trick for the hosts is to continue the theme throughout all the different elements of the party – including not only the costumes but also the invitations, the food, the drinks, the music and the decorations – which is where you come in.

A themed party doesn't have to be expensive. What you need is not so much money as a vivid imagination and a wealth of ideas. You'll probably be surprised, in fact, at all the things you already have in your house – not forgetting those areas of the house where the 'junk' tends to accumulate, like the attic, the spare room and the garden shed – which will come in useful for the decorations or costumes.

You might, for example, decide to focus your party on a colour theme. Throw a Blue party – at which everyone has to wear blue, all the food is blue, the drinks are blue, the music consists of the blues, and all the decorations are blue. Or, following exactly the same principles – clothes, food, drinks, music, accessories – you could equally well have a Pink party, a Purple party, a Green party, a Black party – whatever ... You are only limited by the colours of the rainbow – and there are plenty of them!

Or you might like to take a decade as your theme. Have a 60s party, for example, at which everyone wears mini skirts or sharp suits and the women pile up their hair into beehives and make up their eyes in smudgy black like Dusty Springfield, all the food is inspired by the 60s, the music is made up of 60s revivals led by the Beatles, and the room is decorated in black and white. Alternatively, have a 20s party, or a 40s party, or a 70s party – or whatever most excites your imagination.

Or perhaps you might prefer to be inspired by a particular part of the world. You could have a French café party, for instance, with tables laid with gingham tablecloths, where you serve ham sandwiches and pancakes, and all the guests dress up in bohemian French clothes and listen to Edith Piaf and Charles Aznavour. Or make it a Spanish party, with bullfighters and paella. Or throw a Venetian party, with gondoliers and opera singers. Or you could have a Japanese tea ceremony, at which the guests wear kimonos in minimalist surroundings, eat Japanese delicacies and drink jasmine tea.

Or maybe you could focus on particular characters – say, Vicars and Tarts, Kings and Queens, Cowboys and Cowgirls. Or, instead of people, you might prefer to have an animal theme – say, Cats and Dogs, or a day out at the zoo, or the animals of the jungle. The possibilities are absolutely endless, limited only by the constraints of your imagination.

We have shown you five ideas on the next few pages, but these are only suggestions, not instructions. The hope is that they may prompt you to come up with ideas of your own.

Above all don't be limited by our suggestions – be inspired by them ...

A Sea World Dinner Party

This is a very unusual idea, which really tests the skills of the inveterate fancy dress enthusiast and has a pleasingly comic sense of humour. Decorate the room with imitation seaweed, fishing nets and paper fish or sea horse mobiles, and make a dramatic centrepiece for the table with pebbles and a candle in a jar or alternatively use a bowl full of seashells. Make all the food in the shape of fish – seafood mousse in a fish-shaped mould, for example, followed by a whole fresh salmon and then fish-shaped sweet biscuits served with an octopus-shaped lemon mousse. Finally, offer round a bowl of little shell-shaped chocolates with coffee. Guests can come dressed as anything that springs to mind on a sea theme. They can wear a wet suit, for example, if they have one to hand (though they might get rather hot in the course of the evening!) or they can come dressed as a buoy, or an old wreck, or even in a black bin liner as an oil slick. Play sea shanties or Handel's Water Music in the background, or anything else that you can find in your music collection on an appropriate sea theme.

For a more modern, tasteful alternative ask all your guests to wear aqua, white or grey linen, dress your table to match and serve wine and mussels.

RIGHT • A party is an excellent opportunity to gather together your nearest and dearest friends and family.

ABOVE LEFT • *To ensure a relaxed evening, do as much preparation as possible in advance. A blue decanter, glasses and plates work well together with a checked tablecloth and are in-keeping with a sea theme.*

ABOVE • *Choose a menu that fits in with your sea theme; mussels are easy to prepare and delicious to eat. They can be served in a large bowl, drizzled with lemon juice and everyone can just dig in.*

RIGHT • *Use your imagination to come up with unusual place settings which complement the sea theme. By getting friends involved there will be lots of laughs along the way.*

RIGHT • If you can get hold of a fishing net, try decorating the table by draping it round the edge of a white tablecloth.

BELOW RIGHT • A neutral-coloured linen napkin with raffia, sea shells and pebbles makes a tasteful seascape on your table.

FAR RIGHT • This eye-catching centrepiece is made from pebbles collected from the beach, a glass hurricane lamp and a candle.

The Midsummer Tea Party

Grasp the opportunity of a beautiful hot summer's day to host an elegant midsummer tea party in the open air. This is a particularly good opportunity to invite both ends of the age range in your family or among your social circle, including both the oldest and the youngest, all of whom are sure to have a thoroughly good time. Set up a few pretty tables on the lawn or the patio, and serve endless pots of tea, cucumber sandwiches – with the crusts cut off, of course – brandy snaps and huge blissful chocolate cakes, guaranteed to satisfy even the most demanding chocoholics. The women should wear their best floral summer dresses, and the men should sport elegant linen suits. We can never rely on the weather in this country, so it would be wise to make alternative plans just in case it pours, but an indoor tea party could be just (or almost!) as much fun as long as you're prepared for this eventuality. If you're outside, it may be difficult to set up the music, but 1930s or 40s tea dance music would be both fun and highly appropriate for the occasion. As the afternoon progresses and the younger ones have gone home, why not splash out with some fresh strawberries and a bottle of Champagne for the adults?

ABOVE RIGHT • No tea party is complete without a chocolate cake; seize the opportunity to display it on a cake stand.

RIGHT • Roses are an instant tone-setter for an afternoon party. Place them lavishly in a glass vase to make a lovely centrepiece.

ABOVE • A table laden with strawberries, Champagne glasses and plenty of Champagne is bound to please everyone, regardless of whether the sun is shining or not.

ABOVE RIGHT • Make sure that the teapot never runs dry, slice up plenty of Battenberg cake and you are unlikely to hear many complaints from your guests.

RIGHT • Frosted rose petals, prepared with egg white and caster sugar, have been scattered over this cake to complete the theme.

LEFT • Keep the children happy with fruit-flavoured ice cream – both delicious and cooling on a hot summer's day.

BELOW LEFT • Pick or buy your flowers on the morning of your party so they are still fresh for the event.

RIGHT • An outdoor tea party (weather permitting) is a wonderful way of celebrating a summer birthday.

The Oriental Buffet

An Oriental theme gives plenty of scope, both for guests to dress up and for the hosts to decorate their home. Use hessian and bamboo to your heart's content and serve dim sum, or Chinese dumplings, which you can either make yourself (see page 182) or buy ready-made from most good supermarkets, many of which sell Oriental selections for just such an event. Serve food in traditional Oriental bowls and arrange chopsticks and napkins, tied together with a festive ribbon. Clementines make unusual candleholders and will release a lovely citrus aroma: simply make a hole deep enough to hold a candle and decorate around the base with bay leaves, sprigs of pine or other evergreen leaves. Make a stunning centrepiece for your table with exotic fruit, such as clementines (preferably with their leaves still intact), kumquats, mangoes and physalis, arranged in a huge bowl with coloured glass baubles and a selection of evergreen leaves. It's a good idea to design your centrepiece first and make everything else fit in around it. Alternatively, an unusual idea would be to put a large clear glass bowl in the centre of the table, with a goldfish swimming around in it. Serve Japanese wine or dry white wine, and follow with jasmine tea. Guests can wear Chinese silk pyjama suits or kimonos, as they prefer, or any other Oriental garb that they can pick up in an Oriental supermarket or a second-hand shop, and women should put a silk flower behind each ear.

ABOVE RIGHT • As the host or hostess you should set an example by dressing for the occasion.

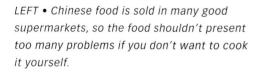

ABOVE • Chinese paper dragons can be found in many good Oriental shops. They are inexpensive and great for parties.

LEFT • Chinese food is sold in many good supermarkets, so the food shouldn't present too many problems if you don't want to cook it yourself.

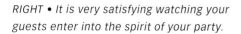

RIGHT • It is very satisfying watching your guests enter into the spirit of your party.

LEFT • A noodle party is stylish, fun and modern, and will be enjoyed by all your guests young and old alike.

BELOW LEFT • Serve a constant supply of either China or jasmine tea, both healthy and very refreshing.

RIGHT • Scour Oriental stores, which are bound to yield plenty of goodies such as banners and lanterns to decorate your party.

A Mexican Dinner Party

Bring the atmosphere of sunny Mexico into your four walls with this unusual themed party, which will be such a lot of fun for all the participants and hosts alike. All the men can dress up as cowboys, with sombreros, bandanas and gaucho boots, and they can grow a crop of real stubble for the occasion and paint on curly moustaches and a few dangerous-looking scars with carefully applied face paint. The women can wear sexy, flamboyant, Spanish-style dresses with frills round the bottom, and show a lot of leg in fancy tights and shiny high heels. Select rhythmic Spanish music to play in the background, and serve spicy stuffed tortillas with soured cream and guacamole. Arrange colourful striped blankets here and there as throws over the furniture or hang them up on the wall, and decorate the house with little painted pots of spiky cacti, and perhaps paint a suggestion, at least, of a few saddled horses on the walls, or on large cardboard panels which you can lean against the walls.

ABOVE RIGHT • Mexican food calls for plenty of limes, pretty, colourful and delicious.

RIGHT • A colourful mix of flowers for a Mexican table centrepiece.

ABOVE • Homemade place names are so much nicer than anything you can buy. This place setting can be made in seconds. Alternatively you could paint your guests' names on the cactus pots or tie a name tag to a mini bottle of tequila.

RIGHT • Try to find a different cactus for each person. Each pot can also be painted a different colour and decorated, if liked.

LEFT • *A brightly-coloured beaded curtain swept aside makes a grand entrance for the Mexican party hostess.*

BELOW LEFT • *The Mexican napkin calls for bright colours, ribbon and plastic flowers.*

RIGHT • *No Mexican party is complete without a large jug of Margarita.*

BELOW • *Finish off the night with a tequila slammer, some salt and a wedge of lime.*

The 20s Cocktail Party

Cocktail parties were particularly popular in high class society in the 1920s and there's never been a better time for their revival. Tell your guests to come in 20s costumes and you'll be amazed at the result. They'll get busy at their sewing machines or they'll raid second-hand clothes shops and come looking elegant and stylish, like a bunch of extras for a film version of *The Great Gatsby*. The men will wear tails or a casual jacket with wide, well-pressed grey flannel trousers, and the women will wear limp, flowing, fluttering crêpe de Chine or flowered chiffon dresses in a soft blue, misty rose or white, reaching down to the ankles, and head-hugging cloche hats. In the background, you may be able to hear the strains of Dixieland Jazz, and as the evening wears on you might even dance the tango. Your main job, as host of this party, is to prepare a range of colourful cocktails and, if you feel like really splashing out, you might like to buy some elegant cocktail glasses in which to serve them.

ABOVE RIGHT • Decorate the rim of your Margarita glasses with salt, making sure that the salt stays in place by dampening the rim of the glass first with water.

RIGHT • Use an authentic cocktail shaker and make the real thing!

FAR RIGHT • A large bowl of punch is great for everyone to help themselves.

LEFT • Exotic fruit is perfect for decorating cocktails and fruit punches.

ABOVE • A Champagne tower looks festive and extravagant.

LEFT • Miniature cocktail parasols are useful for spearing olives and slices of lemon, and they also add colour to your cocktails.

RIGHT • If you are holding your party outside, sparklers add a bit of fun to the occasion.

Allowing People to Talk

The main point of many social occasions is to give the guests the opportunity to strike up a conversation – either with people they see regularly, or with friends they know well but haven't seen for a long time, or with those they've never met before, and music may not be conducive to this. This is particularly so at a buffet party, where many people in the room will be talking at the same time and music may interfere with the acoustics and make it harder for people to hear one another. For this reason, you may prefer to play music as the guests arrive, to provide a gentle, busy noise when there are not many people and the room might otherwise sound empty, and then to turn it off when the party is in full swing. Similarly, at a dinner party, you may decide to play some quiet music at the beginning – over the sherry, say – just to provide atmosphere before any has had the chance to develop of its own accord, and then switch it off during dinner when the conversation has become animated. You could then reintroduce some music over coffee, when things are perhaps winding down in preparation for people to leave. All these decisions are up to you, but they are important and you should think about them and make an informed choice.

The music you choose will probably depend on the guests you have invited. In many instances, you will know their tastes in music, or at least, if they're about the same age as you, you can probably safely assume that their musical tastes are similar to yours. However, at parties such as large family gatherings, where there are many people of different ages, your choice will not be as simple as this. Musical taste is a very personal thing, and you don't want to upset any section of your guests – neither the oldest nor the youngest – by playing what they consider to be the 'wrong' thing throughout the party. If you want to be sure that everyone is getting their say in the choice of music, you could ask people to bring a favourite CD with them – a bit like bringing a bottle – so that everyone gets a crack of the whip. After all, they can't complain that they didn't like all the

music, as long as they have been responsible for their share of the selections. Failing that, you could buy one or two of the ready-mixed CDs and party tapes that are readily available from record shops, covering a deliberately broad spectrum of musical styles.

The Importance of Music

If you decide that you would like to play music at your party, you must think carefully about what and when. It's important to get it right and, above all, it should be memorable. Perhaps most important of all, it should be in

keeping with the general atmosphere of the party and, of course, to the liking of your guests. There's such an enormous variety of musical styles to choose from – classical, jazz, rock, folk, country, piano, big band, orchestral, string quartets, barbershop quartets, or even Elizabethan minstrels – that your main problem is probably that you are going to be spoiled for choice. But for most events, it's important not only to choose carefully but also to plan ahead – at least in principle if not in the tiniest detail – so that the music runs smoothly and without hesitation throughout. This may not be such an issue at a small, casual event – a simple dinner party for close friends, for example, with whose

ABOVE • If you ask your friends to bring their own CDs they can be guaranteed to enjoy some of the music at least! Be sure you know who owns which ones.

LEFT • Encourage musical friends to provide some of the entertainment at your party.

musical tastes you will no doubt be familiar – but for a larger or more formal affair, the choice of music needs careful thought and discussion with everyone involved.

Above all, the music should enhance the whole event. It should play an active role, certainly, in creating the atmosphere that you're seeking to conjure up, perhaps by helping to underline the theme of the party. So if you're having a party on an Oriental theme, for example, you can play Oriental music; or if you're planning a twenties party, say, you should play a selection of 1920s jazz throughout the evening; or if you're planning a party on a blue theme, perhaps – you might extend the theme into the music by playing the blues in the background throughout the evening.

How Loud?

Something else you may worry about is how loud you should play music. This is a difficult decision, and it's easy to get it wrong. It's never easy to please all of the people all of the time, and what is almost certain is that there are always people who would like the music louder, and others who would like it softer. Your problem is finding a happy compromise. It's worth bearing in mind, though, that music doesn't have to be loud to be enjoyable, and music at a deafening level is bound to be too loud for most people. But nor, on the other hand, does it have to be so quiet as to be frankly inaudible. What it does have to be is the right volume, and this is where the difficulty lies. One solution is to confine loud music to one area – perhaps just one room – so that guests can move away from it if it is too noisy for them and they would like some peace and quiet, allowing them to hear themselves – not to mention others – speak. Splitting the party into two separate rooms may spoil the overall atmosphere of the occasion, though the plus side, which is to give both sides of the camp what they want, may be worth it.

If you have neighbours nearby, you may be anxious not to disturb them. It is most imperative in this situation to give your neighbours advance warning that there might be a lot of noise. Once they know, they probably won't mind, as long as it is not something you make a habit of doing too often. If you get on well with your neighbours, perhaps the most diplomatic thing to do would be to invite them to come along – then they'd be an integral part of the noise, not just the victims of it, and they'd be unlikely to object.

Hiring a Disc Jockey

Employing a professional disc jockey is probably the best thing to do if you want your guests to dance and you have plenty of room for this. This is the preferred choice of party for a lot of young people. If you don't know anyone who can give you a personal recommendation, look in the Yellow Pages under Disco – Mobile.

A DJ needs a lot of time to set up – because of the need to get the sound system and the lighting right – so he or she can end up being a lot more expensive than you expected, though probably less expensive than a live band. A DJ creates a rather more intimate atmosphere than a band, which may come as a surprise to you, but in fact it's understandable because there's only one person communicating with the party-goers, rather than a group of them.

Unless you want to give the DJ completely free rein – which is always slightly risky – it's a good idea to spend a little time with him or her in advance, to talk about the kind of music you would like and to discuss the mood and atmosphere that you want to create, otherwise

it may be difficult for him or her to judge the mood of the party and they may so easily get it wrong. You, after all, know the people who are coming and are probably familiar with their musical tastes.

You can also hire someone who will organize a karaoke, at which guests mime or sing to their favourite songs. Karaokes are very popular, as is borne out by the fact that karaoke is listed in the Yellow Pages. They used to be very expensive because of the price of the equipment involved, but they are now more reasonable and within a lot of people's reach.

Hiring a Band

If you are having a large party and you intend dancing to play a major part in the festivities, you may even want to go to the expense of hiring a live band – perhaps a semi-professional function band, say – for the evening. There are many different kinds of musicians or bands available, including five- or seven-piece bands, jazz bands, brass bands, barbershop quartets and a lot of classical musicians, including chamber orchestras, string quartets and even madrigal choirs.

Just think of your favourite kind of music and you're almost bound to find someone who will play it at your special event. Think of your budget, too, and stick to it. You will probably be able to find the kind of music you want by looking up Entertainment or Musicians in the Yellow Pages.

If you decide to employ live musicians and you want to see what you're going to get for your money, you may be able to insist on having a preview before you make a firm choice. It's important to talk to them in advance about who you're inviting and what kind of music would be appropriate. If you're having a mixed group of guests of different ages and with different tastes, you will want a band with a wide repertoire. You will also have to think about what breaks they need from playing, and make your arrangements accordingly. You may have to provide alternative music during their rest periods. If you're planning a really large event

and you've got a lot of money at your disposal, you may like to choose several different acts – a discotheque for background music and to finish the evening, say with a live band as the centrepiece and maybe something else – an entertainer, perhaps – earlier on.

Dancing

If you're throwing your party in a function room somewhere, they're bound to have a special dance floor, but if you're giving it at home, you may feel the need to have a special-purpose wooden dance floor laid temporarily in the centre of the room. A dance floor is obviously an optional extra and is very expensive, but it is sure to create a special, intimate effect, which is ideal for a special evening.

Other Types of Entertainment

People are always looking for original and ever newer ways of entertaining their guests and this is where professional party planners may be able to help you. There are a lot of entertainers who are used to dealing with parties and are expert at making a party gel. The best starting point probably is to look in the Yellow Pages under Entertainment and Entertainment Agencies.

You may associate magicians, for example, with children's parties, but they also perform at a lot of adult parties and can provide highly skilled entertainment to a very high standard. They can do 'table work' at sit-down functions, for example, with card tricks, disappearing acts and sleight of hand.

There are also many other entertainers who offer all sorts of different acts. There are those who will act out a play, clowns, jugglers, comedians, strip shows, and strippergrams (though these are more suitable for parties that take place in a pub or club than for private parties), and entertainers who will also organize a murder mystery, the idea being that the guests then solve the crime. There are people, too, who

organize theme nights, after-dinner speakers, stag and hen nights, and games of bingo.

There are caricaturists or portrait artists who mingle discreetly among the guests and sketch people without them knowing. The high spot of the evening is when the pictures are shown to everyone – including the unsuspecting model, who gets to take the picture home. There are also kissagrams and look-alikes, who are hired, often, as the answer to someone's dream – say the birthday girl has a thing about a particular film actor, and his double comes to give her a passionate kiss at a prearranged time, so causing much mirth and jollity – not to say a good measure of embarrassment for the girl!

The Millennium is probably on your mind, and what better time will there ever be than this to consider the future? You've no time to lose, so seize the occasion and throw a Millennium party, complete with fortune-tellers, crystal gazers, tarot readers, astrologers and palmists. This will be a party you won't forget in a hurry!

ABOVE • Gold and glitter add to the fun of a party. They help to set the mood and create the right atmosphere.

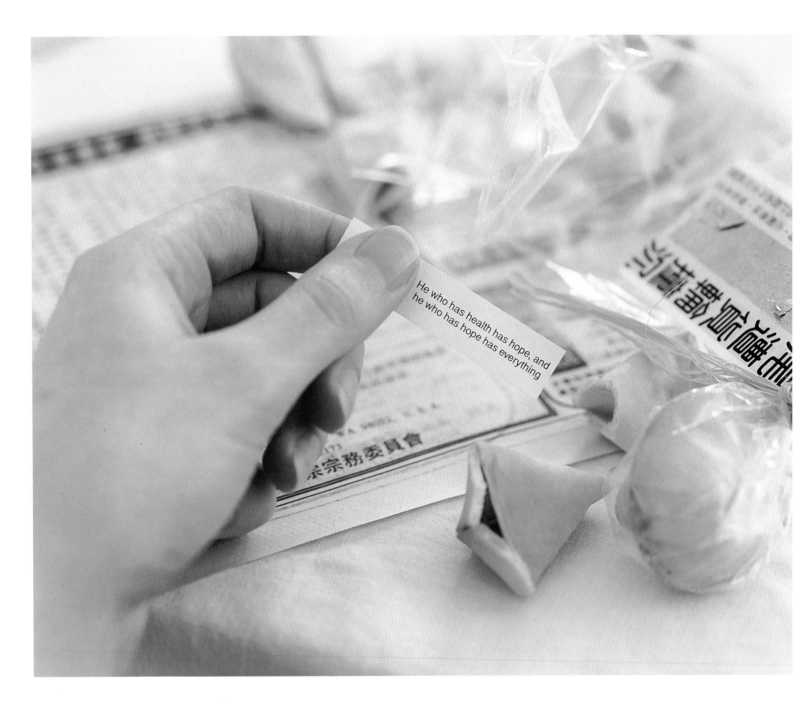

He who has health has hope, and he who has hope has everything

Games

There are a great many silly games – the sillier the better, in fact – that a lot of people enjoy playing at parties. It's amazing how much laughter – not to say hysteria – these can cause and parties are, after all, all about having fun. Lots of fun . . .

There are a great many guessing and memory games. Some games involve all the

ABOVE • Chinese fortune cookies can be used to make part of a novel place setting at a dinner party, particularly one with a Millennium or fortune-telling theme.

RIGHT • Blindman's Buff isn't just for children – it's a good game for adult parties, too, and doesn't embarrass people who feel self-conscious playing acting games.

RIGHT • These red plastic hearts are a reliable guide to the state of the heart and affairs of love. (You can buy them from any joke shop and they come with full instructions.)

FAR RIGHT • Spin the Bottle is one of the many games on the truth, dare or promise theme. The spinner questions whoever the neck of the bottle faces. Then it's that person's turn to spin the bottle.

guests using a piece of paper and a pencil – so if you're going to be playing any of these make sure you have a plentiful supply of pencils and paper ready for everyone in advance.

Charades is an old favourite. Most people tend to lose their inhibitions after a few drinks and this can make for a particularly funny game of mime and guessing. People can either play as individuals, or in teams.

Other possible games include:
• a home version of Call my Bluff, in which people guess the meaning of a word from a choice of three possible answers.
• Consequences, which is a very funny game in which people make up part of a story, write it on a piece of paper and fold over all but the very last words and pass the paper on for another person to write the next instalment.
• Botticelli, in which people have to guess the name of a famous person, either real or fictional, and get there by asking 20 questions, to which the answer can only be yes or no.
• Granny Went to Market, a memory game involving Granny's ever-expanding shopping list.
• Pass the Parcel, in which a parcel is passed from hand to hand until the music stops when the person holding the parcel pulls off as much of the wrapping as they can until the music starts again, with the contents of the parcel going to the person who finally unwraps them.
• Musical Chairs, another game with music in the background.

Another fun idea is to buy a bagatelle board for the occasion – you won't regret it and you'll use it again and again. It's rather like an upmarket, old-fashioned wooden pinball machine, and a lot of merriment is guaranteed for all the assembled company.

You must bear in mind, however, that games are not everyone's cup of tea. It's therefore wise to check with your guests how they feel about games before asking them to join in – maybe

even before they arrive. Some people really don't like playing games – perhaps they feel too inhibited or silly, or games are just not their style – and you should never force anyone to join in against their will, or you can be quite sure that they'll never come to a party of yours again!

Gifts

Small children expect to be given goody bags to take home after a party, and this practice is sometimes also extended to adult parties. They add a nice touch and make people feel special and appreciated, which is something everyone enjoys, whatever their age.

If a special cake was baked for the party – perhaps to mark a birthday, wedding, anniversary, bar mitzvah or christening – then a slice of cake may be enough to serve the purpose, wrapped prettily in special paper or aluminium foil and tied with a ribbon.

Other inexpensive gifts that people can take home as a memento of a party include chocolates, a small tablet of soap, or a miniature bottle of liqueur. If it's Christmas time and you have a Christmas tree, a nice idea is to ask people to choose one of the presents hanging on the tree. These need not be expensive, but

there is something about the ritual of taking the gift off the tree that makes it both seasonal and fun, as well as providing a sense of mystery at the time because people won't know until they get home – or until Christmas Day, perhaps, if they've got the patience – what it is that they've been given in their little parcel.

ABOVE • An enticing package, wrapped in pretty paper and tied with a fancy ribbon, makes a thoughtful way to present a gift to your guests.

ABOVE • Brightly-coloured cellophane or tissue paper are the best wrappings for awkwardly-shaped items such as chocolates or homemade sweets.

Liquid Refreshments

Whatever you're serving at your party – be it a few chilled beers, a wonderful fruit punch, a well-chosen wine or a cup of tea – it is important to realize that the drinks that you offer deserve every bit as much attention as the food.

Planning the Drinks

The drinks that you serve will probably be dictated by two separate and equally important things: first, the type of party you are having; and second, the drinking patterns of your guests, which will probably be influenced by their age, temperament and social habits – all things with which you will probably be familiar. Some of your friends, for example, may be teetotallers, others may only drink wine, say, or perhaps whisky, while others still are perfectly happy to drink absolutely anything that is put in front of them. But in the end it is most likely to be the type of party you are having that will be the deciding factor. The one simply follows the other. This is to state the obvious and it goes, perhaps, without saying. If you're having a cocktail party, for example, you will obviously serve cocktails, with a choice of exciting and colourful concoctions, both alcoholic and non-alcoholic ones for the teetotallers, the drivers and the children.

If you're giving a drinks party, you can serve just about anything you like. Basically, you have two main choices – you can stick to wine – say, a choice of red or white, either still or sparkling, or you can offer a full bar with a choice of spirits and mixers, plus the usual non-alcoholic options for non-drinkers. It is true, however, that in these health-conscious days, a full bar is now much less commonplace than it used to be. That it's not fashionable is not to say that it's wrong, though, and in the end you must choose to do whatever you would prefer.

If you fancy yourself as a bartender and you would like to offer a wide choice of drinks, that's fine. But on the whole, most people these days really do not want to be offered a wide choice of different drinks and, as a general rule, it is often best to keep things as simple as possible. This

has several major advantages: it will not only make life a lot easier for you (and your helpers, if you have any), but it will also greatly help your budget. Entertaining can be an expensive business and this is one way in which you can save money.

If you're giving a formal dinner party, you may offer a range of drinks as the evening wears on. You may start with an apéritif before the meal and then you will probably offer wine throughout the meal – perhaps white to start with, followed by red and then maybe a sweet dessert wine to finish, though the details depend on the menu and there are no hard-and-fast rules. Port with the cheese and a liqueur after the meal with coffee are optional extras, which are perhaps more likely at the smarter, more elaborate end of the dinner party spectrum.

At a buffet party, which is a busy, bustling occasion with no particular specified starting time, where people come and go more or less as they please, the simplest options are probably the best. You might therefore restrict the choice of liquid refreshment to wine throughout the entire evening – except, of course, for non-drinkers, who can drink mineral water. Offer a straightforward choice of red or white wine, depending on what people are eating, and leave it at that.

Whatever you decide to do, though, don't forget, in your haste, to cater for those who don't drink alcohol, as well as those who do normally drink alcohol but who are driving and, being responsible citizens, would therefore prefer to restrict themselves to soft drinks. A cold and constant supply of mineral water and fruit juices or non-alcoholic or low alcohol wines and beers is therefore essential.

A lot of people used to be reluctant – embarrassed, even – to drink non-alcoholic drinks. This is no longer the case and people don't feel that they *have* to drink alcohol. Mineral water is a fashionable, healthy thing to have on offer, anyway, and it's considered perfectly acceptable nowadays for people to ask for a glass of sparkling water with some ice cubes, and perhaps a twist of lemon or lime. The big advantage is that you can sip at your glass

for ever, at no cost to your liver, your head or your driving licence. A lot of people nowadays like to drink water as well as wine throughout a meal, as this both helps to keep their heads clear as well as warding off any morning-after hangover.

Choosing Wine

Wine-making is a great art and is revered by many people the world over. It is a subtle alchemy of a great many interacting factors, including the kind of grape used, the soil in which the vines are grown and and, of course, the climate.

Wine is produced in astonishing abundance – more than 30,000 million bottles of wine every year – which amounts to an awful lot of fermented grape juice. Some of it is excellent, a great deal of it is good, much of it is pretty indifferent and some of it is, quite frankly, downright bad. However, once you get to understand wine and to discover its fascinating variety, you will soon realize why it is one of the truly great civilized pleasures of life.

Britain has a long history of importing wine from all over the world, not only from European countries such as France, Italy and Germany but also New World producers such as Australia, New Zealand, California, South America and South Africa. The result is that we, in this country, are spoiled for choice. We can find wines from all sorts of countries, and at all sorts of different prices, which can become very confusing. Which wine are you most likely to enjoy, you may wonder, what can you afford, which wine goes best with which food, and which offers you the best value for money?

There are many reasons why you might select a particular bottle of wine. You can choose by price, for instance, or by country, or the wily connoisseur may simply choose by nothing more than the variety of grape from which it was made, or you can decide according to the food that you'll be eating with it.

It's not so long ago that there were very strict rules about what wine to drink with which food – it was white wine with fish and red wine with

meat. But now that there are so many wines to choose from and the food we eat has changed this old-fashioned idea has become partially redundant, and people have become much more relaxed and happy to experiment. As long as you take the following considerations into account, your guests will be happy to go along with whatever you choose. Pick a robust wine to accompany robust flavours, and a lighter wine for lighter dishes: neither the food nor the wine should dominate the other. In addition to this, wine should also complement or contrast with a dish in terms of both flavour and texture. A creamy dish could be accompanied by a creamy wine, such as an oaked Chardonnay, or a fresher wine like a Riesling, to add a note of contrast. It is a good idea to think in terms of cooking. A fresh, dry wine will have the same effect as a squeeze of lemon, while a fruity red will add a note of sweetness.

ABOVE • Faced with shelf after shelf of bottles in wine merchants, off-licences and supermarkets, it is sometimes almost impossible to know which wine to choose.

RIGHT • Dessert wines are much under-valued. One of the sweeter German Rieslings would go particularly well with fresh fruit.

The most festive wine, which is perfect for just about any special occasion, is, of course, Champagne. There is an enormous price difference between vintage Champagnes and non-vintage bottles, but the less expensive ones are no less festive for all that, so there is really no need to break the bank. At the bottom end of the market, sparkling wines can also contribute to the festivity of the occasion at a much lower price and are therefore worth considering.

Sparkling wines to try include Veuve de Vernay, Saumur and sweeter Italian versions such as Asti Spumante.

Finding Out About Wine

Learning about wine is not something that you can do just like that, overnight. Unless you follow a special course, it is a long, >page 108

ABOVE • The oaky flavour of Californian Chardonnay makes a brilliant match with smoked salmon.

RIGHT • South American wines are a very good buy at the moment. Serve a Chilean Cabernet Sauvignon with steak and a salad.

Tasting Wines

Tasting wine is, above all, a lot of fun. It is what wine is all about, and what one is meant to do with it, using three of the most important senses – sight, smell and taste. There's no mystery about tasting. It's a straightforward process and just a matter of practice, and you can try at home, quite easily, with your friends and a few bottles of different wines.

Sight

Check for colour, clarity and intensity. Hold the glass at an angle against a white background and assess the colour, especially at the rim – the lightening at the rim comes with age in red wines. Is the wine bright and healthy (a good sign) or cloudy and hazy (not good)? Is it deep or pale? In general, the lighter the colour, the lighter the wine is likely to be.

Smell

Swirl the wine in the glass and check the intensity, health and character of the wine. Is the smell or 'nose' – it's known as the aroma in young wines and the bouquet in mature wines – pronounced, or is it weak? Does it smell clean and pleasant, or is it musty (which could indicate that it is corked, or 'off') and dusty and does it smell of bad eggs? Most people find it difficult to describe the character at first, but soon learn to differentiate between various fruit and flower characteristics, such as raspberry, apple, blackcurrant, peaches, honey, nuts and oak, rose petals, may blossom and elderflower.

Taste

Take a sip of wine and swirl it gently around your mouth. As you do this, take account of all the following factors. Assess the dryness or sweetness of the wine. Note, too, its acidity, which does not mean it's sour but is rather a positive element in a good wine and stops it being flabby (though too much can make the wine tart). Determine its tannin content (this is the substance that makes young red wines seem harsh and astringent – as the wine ages and the tannin comes out, it tastes more mellow). Check its weight or body (German whites feel light, French reds big and heavy). Ascertain the level of alcohol (high alcohol wines warm the tongue, while low alcohol wines are more refreshing). Discover the fruit (both the level and kind). Notice the length (how long the flavour lingers in the mouth after spitting or swallowing – the longer it lasts, the better the wine). And finally, measure the balance (a good wine tastes just right when all the various components are in perfect proportion, especially the balance between sugar and acidity in white wines, fruit and tannin in red: none of these elements should ever be over-obtrusive). Now, draw your conclusions. Is the wine a good example of its kind or a bit run-of-the-mill? Is it ready to drink now or would it be better to wait for a while? Finally, was it worth what you paid for it?

LEFT • First, examine the appearance of the wine, holding the glass in front of a white background and tilting it at an angle.

RIGHT • Smell comes next. Swirl the wine in the glass and check the 'nose'.

FAR RIGHT • Finally, take a sip of the wine and assess its main characteristics.

slow process, which you can only really pick up over the years. A good way of doing this in a systematic way is to buy one or two bottles of different wines at a time, and to make a note in a notebook of the type and year of each one. Then, when you taste it, add your comments about it and perhaps those of any of the people who are sharing it with you. This procedure will enable you, gradually, to build up a sound knowledge of the subject and, in the process, a selection of wines that will suit all occasions.

Many off-licences hold wine tastings, where you can taste wines with which you're not familiar. Others allow their customers to taste the wines that they're thinking of buying, though this may apply only to those in a certain price range.

An Adventure

Don't be afraid of experimenting or of trying something new. Above all, be positively adventurous. This applies especially to inexpensive wines – say, to those under £3.99 or £4.99 – where, if you try the new names on the shelves, from South America and Eastern Europe in particular, you may discover some truly excellent bargains.

If you are still not sure which wine to buy, do not be afraid to ask the people in your local wine shop. Most wine merchants are voluble and enthusiastic about wine, only too prepared to talk about it at some length and to offer you the benefit of their knowledge and wisdom. They really do enjoy helping their customers.

RIGHT • Bulgarian Cabernet Sauvignon is one of the Eastern European wines worth keeping an eye open for. Here it is served in a traditional Paris goblet.

Which Wines Go With What Foods

The chart below is a guide to which types of wine go best with which types of food, though people are more flexible about this now, as they are about many of the conventions surrounding the general subject of wine.

Which Wines Go With What Foods

	Crisp dry white	Medium dry white	Sweet white	Champagne	Light red	Medium red	Full-bodied red	Rosé
Cold hors d'oeuvre	*			*				*
Hot hors d'oeuvre	*	*			*			
Soup	*				*			*
Cold fish	*			*				*
Hot fish	*	*						*
Poultry	*				*	*		
Duck and game						*	*	
Red meat						*	*	
Pork					*	*		
Cheese					*	*	*	
Dessert		*	*	*				
Fruit		*		*				

Storing Wine

The principles you should follow for storing wine vary little, whether you are laying down a grand, valuable wine for drinking in a few years' time or you are putting away a mixed selection of inexpensive wines to be drunk with your friends in a few days' time. Generally speaking, all wines improve to some extent when they are kept, or 'laid down', for a while, though some improve rather more than others.

It is particularly important, for example, for fine clarets and for red and white burgundies. It also does a favour to some of the finest red wines from Italy, Spain, California and South America, as well as white wines from Bordeaux and the sweeter dessert wines from Germany. The lighter red wines, on the other hand, as well as the fruity dry white wines are not really meant to be kept. They are designed rather to be drunk 'young' and do not really benefit greatly from keeping.

The best conditions for keeping wine are those found in a cellar, but few people nowadays are lucky enough to have a cellar, in which case a dark cupboard, where the temperature is constantly cool at around 10–12°C/50–55°F, will serve the purposes just as well. The space below the stairs is another favourite in many houses for storing wine, while some people make a sort of cupboard, if there's room for it, under the floorboards, which doesn't require a great deal of effort and works perfectly well.

Excessive heat will cause the wine to get hot and expand – in which case it may seep through the cork and from under the capsule. Too much light will lead to oxidation. Above all, avoid keeping wine anywhere that is close to a boiler or radiator, or where there is a particularly strong draught from a door to the outside, as wine does not like sudden or extreme fluctuations in temperature.

There are a few simple rules that you can follow for keeping wine.
• Do make sure that the room where you keep your wine is clean and dry. A musty, damp room could cause the cork to rot – though many wines now have synthetic corks.
• Keep wine away from direct sunlight – this makes it age too quickly and oxidize. It also ruins the labels.
• Ideally, wine bottles with corks should be stored horizontally, particularly if you are intending to keep them for longer than three months. The reason for this is that the wine is constantly in contact with the cork, which prevents it from drying out, contracting, or allowing air to get into the bottle.
• Use purpose-made wine racks, which are a practical and convenient way of storing your wine.
• Screw-cap bottles can be stored upright – and it may be most convenient to keep them in the cardboard box in which they originally came from the shop.

What's in a Bottle?

Most wines are sold in standard 75 cl bottles. Half-bottles are 37.5 cl and hasten ageing because they contain more oxygen per centilitre. For the last 300 years – ever since the technology was developed to make glass in commercial quantities – wine has been stored and served in glass bottles (pottery and stoneware jugs were used before that).

Bottles are relatively heavy and inconveniently fragile. They are also portable, protective and, most important as far as ageing is concerned, entirely odourless and inert.

There are basically four different types of wine bottle:
• The traditional Bordeaux bottle, with its square shoulders, has become the classic shape for maturing fine red wines all over the world. It has a punt – an indentation in the bottom of the bottle – which adds strength and helps catch sediment. Dark green glass is used for reds and some dry whites; clear glass is used for most dry and sweet whites; and brown is used by producers of Chianti.
• The Burgundy bottle has sloping shoulders and a punt. Yellow-green glass is used for both red and white wines.
• The tall slender bottle, or flute, used for German wines, does not have a punt. Wines from the Rhine are bottled in brown glass; Mosel and Alsace are bottled in green glass; and Loire rosés are bottled in clear glass.
• The heavy Champagne bottle has a deep punt and a lip for the wire muzzle which holds the cork in place. The dark green glass is thick, as it needs to withstand the pressure created by sparkling wine, and is also resistant to light, which could make the wine oxidize.

Modern Trends

Nowadays, wine is also available in cans, plastic bottles and boxes. Boxed wines, which have become universally popular for picnics and parties, are an Australian invention, and a convenient way of storing and selling table wines. The wine is vacuum-sealed in a plastic bag packed inside a cardboard box, and supplied with a plastic tap. The vacuum causes the bag to collapse as the wine is consumed, preventing air from reaching it.

Despite the convenience of new forms of packaging, such as boxes, cans and plastic containers, wine in fact lasts longer and ages far better in a traditional glass bottle with a cork. Glass doesn't affect the taste of the wine, no matter how long it is stored.

RIGHT • Wine bottles vary in colour as well as in shape. Red wines generally come in green bottles, while white wines are found in green, brown and clear bottles, depending on where they originate from; rosés are also bottled in clear glass. The Champagne bottle is much stronger than the others, to withstand the pressure of the secondary fermentation in the bottle.

Opening Wine Bottles

Most wines can be opened an hour or two in advance, and many will, in fact, improve if this is done. Champagne, however, should not be opened until just before it is served, so if you need a lot for a special toast, you will need to enlist some help.

To open a bottle of still wine, simply wipe the neck of the bottle with a clean, damp cloth to remove any dust or dirt. Then remove the capsule sealing the top of the bottle – you can buy a little gadget for this. Now, using a good corkscrew, draw the cork slowly and evenly from the neck of the bottle.

Corkscrews made of boxwood with two threads turning in opposite directions are very reliable. Some corkscrews inject air into the bottle to force the cork out. The best ones ease the cork out vertically. A simple screwpull is fine, and so are the lever varieties. But, that said, a round, not chisel-edged, screw is the very best. It's a good idea to have more than one corkscrew to hand, as they are notoriously easy to mislay and it can cause consternation when one can't be found.

Most people believe that there's no need to decant young wines, though it must be said that a cheap red wine can look much more special if it is decanted, and this seems to have the psychological effect of making it taste better. It is only during the ageing process of old wines that a natural deposit may be found in the bottle of a good, well-made red. To decant an old wine, gently lift the bottle from the rack and, keeping it horizontal, place it in a decanting basket. Remove the cork and carefully pour the wine into the decanter in a slow, steady stream until you can see the deposit at the neck of the bottle. Stop pouring the wine as soon as you see the deposit.

LEFT • A selection of corkscrews. Just behind the very effective modern screwpull is a wooden corkscrew of the type in use in the 1920s. The brush was for removing fragments of dust, wax or cork after the sealing wax had been removed from the bottle but before the cork was drawn.

It may be fun to shake a bottle of bubbly, open it and spray the fizz all over the place, just like the victorious drivers of racing cars. But it can be dangerous if you hit someone with the cork and is therefore best avoided. It's also a dreadful waste of Champagne. The reason it fizzes so much is because it is under pressure in the bottle and shaking only increases the pressure. The art of opening a bottle of Champagne is to do nothing to increase that pressure. Chilling is essential, and you must keep the bottle very still. Carefully remove the foil and the wire muzzle. Hold your hand over the cork so no one gets hit if it pops unexpectedly. Slowly tilt the bottle to about 30 degrees. Keeping one hand on the cork, hold

ABOVE • The summit of a Champagne tower. To perform this party trick, arrange five wide Champagne glasses in a circle with their rims touching, stand three more on top of them and place one single glass on top. Now pour Champagne into the top glass so that it flows into the second and lower tiers, like a fountain. Turn to page 82 to see the result.

the base of the bottle with your other hand. Gently twist the bottle with the hand holding the base, keeping the hand that is holding the cork absolutely still. As you twist, hold the cork steady to stop it flying out. When you slowly turn the bottle, you will see and hear a slight fizz and the cork will gently pop out of the neck.

You can buy stoppers to reseal wines. Some of these involve evacuating the bottle of all its air, which keeps the wine fresh for longer. You can buy stoppers for Champagne, too, but one of the most effective ways of keeping the wine sparkling is to put an upturned silver spoon in the neck of the bottle, and then to chill it. It will keep its bubbles for 12 hours.

Serving Wine

People are becoming increasingly flexible, too, as they are about so much to do with wine, about the temperatures at which wine should be served. In general, though, it is best to serve red wines at room temperature, which means about 15–18°C/60–64°F. One of the exceptions to this is Beaujolais Nouveau, which is one of the few red wines that can happily – indeed some would say should – be served chilled. You should usually allow time for wine that is taken from a cool place to reach this optimum temperature gradually.

Dry white wines should be served chilled, at around 7–9°C/45–48°F, and sweet dessert ones slightly more chilled at about 6°C/43°F. Most people agree that if you serve a wine at the wrong temperature, then you ruin all the hard work that's gone into creating the wine.

Conversely, if you serve a wine at the right temperature you can make an average wine seem rather good and a good one taste great.

Both red and white wines will benefit from being opened about an hour before you plan to serve them, except of course sparkling wines. There is some controversy about the need to allow wines to 'breathe', but the general consensus of opinion is that the finer the wine, the more important it is to open it in advance of serving. Thus a good red wine will benefit by being opened at least a couple of hours before serving, and a young red by being given an hour or more to breathe.

Pour in enough wine so that the glass is no more than half full. This is not a silly affectation, far from it. It airs the wine and allows you to enjoy its bouquet.

Apéritifs

The purpose of an apéritif – which is drunk before lunch or dinner – is both to prepare the palate and to whet the appetite. Sherry used to be considered the best – if not the only – apéritif in this country, but there are now many other drinks, including European fortified wines, Madeira, dry Marsala, white port, Dubonnet, Vermouth and Campari. These can all be served over cracked ice, or diluted with a mixer such as soda water or tonic and served with a cube of ice and a twist of orange, lemon or lime.

Champagne or sparkling wine can be a festive apéritif and is nearly always a welcome choice. There seems to be something special about the bubbles. This wine seems to have an almost magical power to lift the spirit, particularly when you're feeling low. Always serve Champagne well chilled, and tilt the glass towards the bottle as you pour it slowly on to the inside of the glass, which makes the most of the bubbles.

Some people, though, find Champagne too acidic and it's therefore a good idea to offer supplies of orange juice (preferably fresh) or Crème de Cassis (a blackcurrant liqueur) so you can give people a Buck's Fizz or a Kir Royale (one part Crème de Cassis to 8 or 10 parts Champagne), plus a non-alcoholic option for the non-drinkers at the party.

Digestifs

These are drunk after dinner. Popular choices include brandies distilled from wine, such as Cognac and Armagnac, and port, which is one of the finest fortified wines in the world.

Other after-dinner drinks include various liqueurs, which are all spirit based and therefore strong, including Grand Marnier, Tia Maria, Chartreuse and Cointreau. They're not to

everyone's taste and a lot of people find them too powerful however– both in alcohol and in their not-too-subtle flavour.

Glasses

A good wine glass is a simple glass. Choose one that is clear, plain and transparent, so you can properly appreciate the colour and clarity of the wine. A glass with a fine rim is more pleasant to drink out of than a thick, heavy-rimmed glass, and the bowl should be large enough to allow the wine to be swirled around with plenty of room to spare.

ABOVE • A selection of glasses for some special occasions. Choose heatproof glasses with handles for mulled wines and hot punches, neat elegant little glasses for liqueurs and glasses with a wide vee-shaped bowl on a long stem for cocktails.

It is usually possible to borrow glasses from the same place that you buy the drinks for your party, in which case you usually pay only for breakages. People have a habit of abandoning their glasses and forgetting where they put them. It's sensible, therefore, to have more glasses than people. Check that you have the correct number and wash them before use.

Which Glass?

If at all possible, it's best to choose your glasses to match the drinks on offer, such as large wine glasses for wine, narrow flutes for Champagne, and straight-sided tumblers for juice and water. Although a good-sized wine glass is perfectly suitable for most drinks, there are some glasses which are associated with particular drinks, and some glasses which are quite simply just a pleasure to use.

The selection above includes the following

1 Liqueur glass: This glass has a very small capacity for holding the most potent drink of all. If your guests like their liqueurs served on ice, you will have to use a larger glass to make room for it.

2 Brandy balloon: Sometimes known as a snifter, this large glass is designed so the bowl is cupped in the hand and gently swirled to warm the brandy.

3 Old-fashioned glass: Originally designed for the classic cocktail of that name, this straight-sided tumbler holds 175–250 ml/6–8 fl oz. A good glass for whisky.

4 Highball glass: A tall straight-sided tumbler holding about 250 ml/8 fl oz. It is ideal for cocktails that are served over ice and topped up with soda water or other mixers.

5 Margarita glass: This oddly-shaped cocktail glass with a small bowl topped by a wide saucer has a wide rim for the salt required by Margarita drinkers.

6 The standard wine glass: This is made in a variety of shapes, narrowing slightly towards the top, and holds about 150 ml/5 fl oz.

7 Hurricane glass: This tall curved glass, shaped like a hurricane lamp, is used for medium to long drinks and cocktails served over lots of ice.

8 Pilsner glass: Originally made for German beer, this glass is suitable for most long drinks.

9 and **10** Champagne flutes: The flute is a tall slim glass with a narrow bowl. This shape allows the bubbles in Champagne and other sparkling wines to develop and prevents them from disappearing too quickly (whereas flat saucer-like glass lets them dissipate much too soon). It holds about 100 ml/3½ fl oz. When you pour Champagne or other sparkling wines into a flute, fill it three-quarters full so you can appreciate the column of bubbles.

11 Classic cocktail glass: This has a vee-shaped bowl set on a long stem.

shaker, which usually has a built-in strainer, is used for drinks which require a thorough shaking; these are the ones which contain ingredients such as egg whites, syrups and fruit. The mixing glass, which is large enough to make several servings of a cocktail at one time, is used for drinks which only require a gentle stirring before they are poured or strained into cocktail glasses. The blender is used for making drinks containing fresh fruit, ice cream and milk; it is particularly useful for smoothies, milk shakes and drinks of that sort. A chopping board, a sharp knife, ice trays for freezing ice and ice containers to hold it and tongs to lift it, a bar strainer and a long-handled bar spoon, a set of bar measures, a corkscrew, a bottle opener and a waiter's friend for coping with stubborn bottles and a large supply of cocktail sticks and tea towels are essentials; a salt saucer if you plan to rim Margaritas, glass swizzle sticks and lots of coloured straws are nice to have around.

Sugar Syrup

This is useful for sweetening cocktails and punches as it blends into cold drinks more quickly than sugar. To make a supply, put 4 tablespoons of caster sugar into a small saucepan with 4 tablespoons of water and bring slowly to the boil, stirring to dissolve the sugar, then boil the mixture without stirring for 1–2 minutes. Sugar syrup can be stored in a sterilized bottle in the refrigerator for up to 2 months.

RIGHT and FAR RIGHT • Cocktails lend themselves to zany decorations. With a supply of cocktail sticks to hand, embellish your drinks with fresh fruit and herb sprigs in whatever combinations take your fancy. Anything goes.

Decorating Cocktails

Some cocktails have time-honoured decorations that cannot be bettered, such as the green olive or lemon rind in a Dry Martini, or the red cherry in a Manhattan. In many cases, though, the decoration depends on what is available, appropriate (an orange slice in an orange-flavoured drink, for example, or a mint sprig floating in a glass of Pimms), and looks attractive.

Occasionally, the glass itself is decorated – rimmed with sugar, perhaps, or with salt for a Margarita. To do this, run a slice of citrus fruit around the top of the glass to moisten it, or dip it into beaten egg white, and then dip the glass into a saucer of caster sugar or salt.

As well as cocktail cherries and olives, decorate your drinks with fresh strawberries (whole or halved), slices of citrus fruit, chunks of pineapple or mango, herbs, especially mint sprigs, and long spirals of orange, lemon and lime rind.

Ice cubes, too, can be made more decorative by freezing single raspberries or mint sprigs inside each cube. Some long drinks are served with one or two coloured straws, while parasols and swizzle sticks are other options.

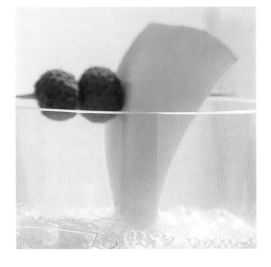

Smoking

Alcohol and cigarettes are often partners and it is an age-old truism that wherever you find people indulging in alcoholic drinks, you will also find people smoking. Smokers are very conscious nowadays that their habit may not be to everyone's liking and, as a result, most of them are a lot better behaved than they used to be. They probably won't grind their butts into your carpets these days, and they may even ask everyone in their vicinity, 'Do you mind if I smoke?' But they probably won't expect anyone to say yes and the question may be no more than surface politeness.

There are some people who won't allow anyone to smoke in their house, and there are others who consider that the way round the problem is to have a 'smoking' room where all the smokers can congregate together and breathe in each other's smoke. What you choose to do is up to you, but if you do allow smoking, always make sure that the smokers have got plenty of ashtrays within easy reach.

Coffee

You can serve coffee at the dining table or adjourn to another part of the room, or even to another room altogether, as you prefer. Sometimes, moving everyone to somewhere different can break up a good conversation, just as it was in full swing, and it can destroy the atmosphere of the party, which can be a great shame if it was going well. Nowadays, a lot of people follow the Continental habit of remaining seated at the table for the rest of the evening, which is a pleasantly sociable thing to do. Have the coffee cups, sugar and milk or cream ready for when they are required, together with a little bowl of mints, after-dinner chocolates or petits fours.

Not everyone can drink coffee late in the evening, as it can prevent some people sleeping, so it is considerate to offer your guests decaffeinated coffee, or perhaps a choice of tea as well, either Indian, China or herbal. Mint is a popular herbal tea, which is a good after-dinner drink as it is said to aid the digestion.

White Russian

left

Serves: **1**

Preparation time: 3 minutes

5 ice cubes, cracked
1 measure vodka
1 measure Tia Maria
1 measure milk or double cream

Put half the ice cubes into a cocktail shaker and add the vodka, Tia Maria and milk or double cream. Shake to mix. Put the remaining ice cubes into a tall narrow glass and strain the cocktail over them. Drink with a straw.

Black Russian

above left

Serves: **1**

Preparation time: 3 minutes

cracked ice
2 measures vodka
1 measure Kahlúa coffee liqueur
chocolate stick, to decorate (optional)

Put some cracked ice into a short glass. Add the vodka and Kahlúa and stir. Decorate with a chocolate stick, if liked.

Moscow Mule

right

Serves: **1**

Preparation time: 5 minutes

2–3 ice cubes
juice of ½ lime
twist of lime rind
1½ measures vodka
ginger beer
TO DECORATE
strip of lime rind
lime slice

Put the ice cubes into a tall glass, add the lime juice and rind and stir in the vodka. Top up with ginger beer and decorate with lime rind and a slice of lime.

Screwdriver

far right

Serves: **1**

Preparation time: 3 minutes

2–3 ice cubes
1 measure vodka
juice of 1 orange

Put the ice cubes into a tumbler. Add the vodka and orange juice, and stir lightly.

Whisky Daisy

below left

Serves: **1**

Preparation time: 3 minutes

3 ice cubes, crushed
1 egg white (optional)
½ measure lemon juice
1 measure Scotch whisky
1 teaspoon pernod
2 dashes grenadine
soda water
lemon rind, to decorate

Put the ice into a cocktail shaker and add the egg white, if using, lemon juice, whisky, pernod and grenadine. Shake to mix. Strain into a tumbler, top up with soda water and decorate with a twist of lemon rind.

Mint Julep

below right

Serves: **1**

Preparation time: 3 minutes

3 mint sprigs
½ teaspoon caster sugar
1 tablespoon soda water
2–3 ice cubes, crushed
1 measure Bourbon whiskey
mint sprig, to decorate

Crush the mint with the sugar in a tumbler and rub it around the sides of the glass. Discard the mint. Dissolve the sugar in the soda water, add the ice and pour over the Bourbon. Do not stir. Decorate with a mint sprig.

Cuba Libre

far right

Serves: **1**

Preparation time: 3 minutes

2–3 ice cubes
1½ measures dark rum
juice of ½ lime
Coca-cola
lime slice, to decorate

Place the ice cubes in a tall tumber and pour over the rum and lime juice. Stir to mix. Top up with Coca-cola, decorate with the lime slice and drink through a straw.

Zombie

right

Serves: **1**

Preparation time: 5 minutes

3 ice cubes, cracked
1 measure dark rum
1 measure white rum
½ measure apricot brandy
2 measures unsweetened pineapple juice
juice of ½ lime
2 teaspoons powdered sugar
TO DECORATE
slice of kiwi fruit
cocktail cherry
pineapple wedge
powdered sugar (optional)

Place a tall glass in the freezer so the outside becomes frosted. Put the ice into a cocktail shaker. Add the rums, apricot brandy, fruit juices and sugar. Shake to mix. Pour into the glass without straining. To decorate, put the kiwi, cherry and pineapple on to a cocktail stick and place it across the top of the glass. Sprinkle the powdered sugar over the top and drink, if liked, with a straw.

Florida Skies

far left

Serves: **1**

Preparation time: 3 minutes

cracked ice
1 measure white rum
¼ measure fresh lime juice
½ measure pineapple juice
soda water
cucumber or lime slices, to serve

Put some cracked ice in a tall glass. Put the rum, lime and pineapple juices into a cocktail shaker. Shake lightly. Strain into the glass and top up with soda water. Serve with the cucumber or lime slices.

Piña Colada

right

Serves: **1**

Preparation time: 5 minutes

cracked ice
1 measure white rum
2 measures coconut milk
2 measures pineapple juice
TO DECORATE
strawberry slice
mango slice
pineapple slice

Put some cracked ice, the rum, coconut milk and pineapple juice into a cocktail shaker. Shake lightly to mix. Strain into a large glass and decorate with the fruit.

Grasshopper

above right

Serves: **1**

Preparation time: 3 minutes

1 measure crème de cacao
1 measure crème de menthe

Pour the crème de cacao into a glass. Pour the crème de menthe gently over the back of a teaspoon so that it floats on top and serve.

Daiquiri

far right

Serves: **1**

Preparation time: 3 minutes

3 ice cubes, cracked
1 measure fresh lime juice
3 measures white rum
1 teaspoon powdered sugar
lime wedge, to serve

Put the cracked ice into a glass. Pour over the lime juice then the rum, add the sugar and stir lightly. Serve with a lime wedge.

Margarita

below left

Serves: **1**

Preparation time: 5 minutes

a little fresh lime juice
finely ground sea salt
1½ measures tequila
1 measure Cointreau
1–2 tablespoons fresh lime juice
cracked ice

Dip the rim of a chilled glass in lime juice, then in the salt. Place the tequila, Cointreau, lime juice and cracked ice in a cocktail shaker. Shake well to mix. Pour into the glass.

Americano

below right

Serves: **1**

Preparation time: 3 minutes

cracked ice
1 measure Campari
2 measures sweet vermouth
soda water
lemon slice, to serve

Put some cracked ice into a tumbler, pour over the Campari and vermouth and stir to mix. Top up with soda water to taste. Serve with a lemon slice.

Tequila Sunrise

right

Serves: **1**

Preparation time: 5 minutes

5–6 ice cubes
1 measure tequila
2½ measures fresh orange juice
2 teaspoons grenadine
TO DECORATE
orange slice
starfruit slice (optional)

Crack half the ice and put it into a cocktail shaker. Add the tequila and orange juice and shake to mix. Put the remaining ice into a tall glass and strain the tequila mixture into the glass. Slowly pour in the grenadine and allow it to settle. Just before serving, stir once. Decorate with the fruit.

Blue Moon

far right

Serves: **1**

Preparation time: 3 minutes

5 ice cubes, cracked
¾ measure vodka
¾ measure tequila
1 measure blue curaçao
lemonade

Put half the ice cubes into a mixing glass and add the vodka, tequila and blue curaçao. Stir to mix. Put the remaining ice into a glass and strain in the cocktail. Top up with lemonade and drink with a straw.

Summer Cup

below left

Serves: **15**

Preparation time: 5 minutes

1 bottle Riesling, chilled
1 bottle light red wine
75 ml/3 fl oz Drambuie
750 ml/1¼ pints lemonade, chilled
1 dessert apple, sliced
1 orange, sliced
a few strawberries, halved
ice cubes
strawberry slices, to decorate

Pour the Riesling, red wine and Drambuie into a large chilled bowl. Add the lemonade, fruit and ice cubes. Serve as soon as possible in glasses decorated with strawberry slices.

Honeysuckle Cup

below right

Serves: **10–12**

Preparation time: 10 minutes, plus chilling

1 tablespoon clear honey
1 bottle medium dry white wine
2 tablespoons Bénédictine
150 ml/¼ pint brandy
750 ml/1¼ pints lemonade, chilled
1 peach, skinned and sliced
seasonal fruit, to decorate

Put the honey into a large bowl and gradually stir in the wine. Add the Bénédictine and brandy. Chill for 2 hours. Just before serving, add the lemonade and fruit.

Brandy Alexander

far right

Serves: **1**

Preparation time: 3 minutes

2–3 ice cubes, cracked
1 measure brandy
1 measure crème de cacao
1 measure double cream
grated nutmeg, for sprinkling

Put the ice into a cocktail shaker and add the brandy, crème de cacao and cream. Shake well to mix thoroughly then strain into a cocktail glass. Sprinkle nutmeg over the top before serving.

Between the Sheets

right

Serves: **1**

Preparation time: 3 minutes

2–3 ice cubes, cracked
½ measure brandy
½ measure white rum
½ measure Cointreau
1 tablespoon fresh orange juice
TO DECORATE
cocktail cherry
orange slice

Put the ice into a cocktail shaker. Add the brandy, rum, Cointreau and orange juice and shake to mix. Strain into a cocktail glass. Decorate with a cocktail cherry and an orange slice on a cocktail stick.

Sangria

left

Serves: **10–12**

Preparation time: 10 minutes

ice cubes
2 bottles light Spanish red wine, chilled
125 ml/4 fl oz brandy (optional)
about 450 ml/¾ pint soda water, chilled
sliced seasonal fruit (apples, pears, oranges,
    lemons, peaches, strawberries)

Put the ice into a large bowl and pour over the
wine and brandy, if using. Stir. Add soda water
to taste and float the fruit on top. Serve in
glasses decorated with an orange slice.

Apple Posset

above left

Serves: **1**

Preparation time: 5 minutes

Cooking time: 2 minutes

200 ml/7 fl oz unsweetened apple juice
1 teaspoon soft brown sugar
2 tablespoons Calvados
5 cm/2 inch cinnamon stick

Heat the apple juice in a small saucepan to
just below boiling point. Meanwhile, measure
the sugar and Calvados into a warmed glass or
mug. Pour the hot apple juice on to the
Calvados, stirring with the cinnamon stick until
the sugar has dissolved.

Siamese Slammer

far right

Serves: **4**

Preparation time: 5 minutes

125 ml/4 fl oz vodka
juice of 2 oranges
1 small ripe papaya, peeled and chopped
1 banana, sliced
juice of 1 lime
125 ml/4 fl oz sugar syrup
ice
papaya slice, to decorate

Put all the ingredients into a blender and blend
until smooth. Serve in a tall glass decorated
with a papaya slice.

Thai Sunrise

right

Serves: **4**

Preparation time: 10–12 minutes

2 ripe mangoes, peeled and sliced
125 ml/4 fl oz tequila
50 ml/2 fl oz Cointreau
25 ml/1 fl oz grenadine
75 ml/3 fl oz lime or lemon juice
75 ml/3 fl oz sugar syrup
6 ice cubes, cracked
TO DECORATE
lime and orange slices
mint sprigs

Put all the ingredients into a food processor
and blend until the ice is crushed. Serve in tall
glasses, decorated with lime and orange slices
and mint sprigs.

Cranberry Crush

right

Serves: **10**

Preparation time: 10 minutes

Cooking time: 5 minutes

600 ml/1 pint cranberry juice
600 ml/1 pint orange juice
150 ml/¼ pint water
½ teaspoon ground ginger
½ teaspoon mixed spice
sugar, to taste
TO DECORATE
kumquats
frosted cranberries
mint sprigs

Place the cranberry and orange juices, water, ginger and mixed spice in a saucepan and bring gently to the boil, stirring in sugar to taste. Simmer for 5 minutes. Pour into punch cups, decorate with kumquats, frosted cranberries and mint sprigs. Serve this drink chilled for a summer party.

Fruit Punch

above right

Serves: **12**

Preparation time: 10 minutes, plus chilling

600 ml/1 pint orange juice
600 ml/1 pint cranberry juice
300 ml/½ pint pineapple juice
250 ml/8 fl oz soda water
ice cubes
TO DECORATE
orange slices
apple slices

Pour the orange, cranberry and pineapple juices and soda water into a large punch bowl or jug and mix well. Leave to chill in the refrigerator until required. To serve, add the ice cubes and decorate with the fruit.

Tenderberry

right

Serves: **1**

Preparation time: 5 minutes

6–8 strawberries
1 measure grenadine
1 measure double cream
1 measure dry ginger ale
crushed ice
a little ground ginger
strawberry, to decorate (optional)

Place the strawberries, grenadine and cream in a food processor with some crushed ice and blend for 30 seconds. Pour into a tumbler. Add the dry ginger ale and stir. Sprinkle a little ground ginger on top and decorate with a strawberry, if liked.

Limeade

far right

If you roll the limes around quite hard on a board with your hand, you will find that you get more juice from them.

Serves: **8**

Preparation time: 6 minutes, plus infusing and chilling

6 limes
125 g/4 oz caster sugar
750 ml/1¼ pints boiling water
pinch of salt
ice cubes
lime wedges, to decorate

Halve the limes then squeeze the juice into a large jug. Put the squeezed halves into a heatproof jug with the sugar and boiling water and leave to infuse for 15 minutes. Add the salt, give the infusion a good stir then strain it into the jug with the lime juice. Add half a dozen ice cubes, cover and refrigerate for 2 hours or until cold. To serve, place 3–4 ice cubes in each glass and pour the limeade over them. Decorate with a lime wedge.

Party Food

Depending on the type of party you're giving, the food may be either insubstantial or it may be considerable. This is the main difference between a drinks party and a dinner party.

In other words, the food may consist of no more than occasional nibbles, which are almost incidental to the drinks and are really just something to add a little interest to the occasion and to soak up some of the alcohol. Don't underestimate the expectations of your guests, however. This food should look appetizing and should be both stylish and tasty. Snacks such as this are known in France as *amuse gueule*, which means, literally, something to entertain the mouth. In this case, the guests will probably either have eaten beforehand, or they will be planning to have a meal afterwards, either when they get home or perhaps, if they are short of time to prepare dinner, at a nearby restaurant.

Alternatively, the food may constitute a complete meal, probably consisting of several substantial courses. If this is a buffet party, there will probably be a main course followed by a dessert, whereas if this is a dinner party, there will be probably also be one or two hors d'oeuvres, though the trend nowadays is for smaller meals. The food can be eaten either standing up, as at a buffet party, or sitting down, as at a sit-down supper, lunch or dinner party at which there are enough chairs for everyone.

The Right Food For the Occasion

It is important to tailor the food to suit the occasion, and this is one of the first things that you'll have to do when you are still at the planning stage.

If you are offering a range of nibbles, for example, you will probably want to offer a selection of savoury finger foods. These can be either hot or cold, depending probably on the time of year – cold savouries are best in summer and hot in winter. There is no need to offer anything sweet, as this is only a snack and not a proper meal. If you're not sure how to calculate the quantities necessary for finger foods, work on the basis of about

8–12 savouries per person. This is a reliable starting point and you can't go very far wrong.

If you're planning a simple buffet, this is likely to consist either of a combination of finger and fork foods, or just fork foods, as you prefer. Again, whether the food is primarily hot or cold will depend on the time of year. It might consist of two or three canapés, followed by a fork dish, one or two salads and a piece of bread, and then one or two cold desserts to finish. Don't forget, whatever it is you're serving, to offer some vegetarian dishes for any vegetarian guests.

Buffet Parties

Buffet parties have the great advantage that they give you the opportunity to entertain more people than you could cater for around a table and, as such, they can be a lot of work but also a corresponding amount of fun.

The food on a buffet table should present your guests with an eye-catching and mouthwatering display, which lures them towards its delights. Plan which serving dishes you want to use in advance, in order to set the foods off to their best possible advantage. Arrange the foods attractively in relation to one another, keeping an eye out for pleasing contrasts of colour and texture, which will add visual interest. If a dish is particularly dull in appearance, make sure you liven it up by putting it next to a bright, colourful one.

Make it easy for people to serve themselves. Flans, pies and tarts, for example, should be cut into portions, which also makes it easier for guests to see how much they should take. Cut terrines and pâtés into slices, and provide cocktail sticks wherever possible to make serving easier.

Remember, too, that the food should be easy to eat with as little cutlery as possible – say, just a fork and never a knife, which would be just too difficult to manage when you are standing or, at best, perching on the back of a sofa or on a cushion.

Dinner Parties

At a dinner party, the food lies at the heart of the evening, and it should always be high on style and low on the need for last-minute attention from the hostess, which would take her away from her guests for too long and could well disrupt both the conversation and the atmosphere.

It is generally best to decide on the main course first of all, choosing something that you have cooked successfully before and that you are therefore confident you can cook well. Don't choose the occasion of a dinner party to experiment. This is not the best time to try a new dish for the first time, which you've never cooked before. It might look great on paper and seem to offer a tempting challenge, but it could equally well be a recipe for disaster. It is best, therefore, to stay with dishes that you've already tried and tested.

Stick to seasonal fruit and vegetables, if possible, rather than being tempted by extravagant, out-of-season produce. Seasonal foods will ease your budget as well as providing the best and freshest flavours. Seasonal doesn't have to be boring – that depends, quite simply, on what you do with it.

Remember that a 'starter' is just that. It is not intended to satisfy the appetite, merely to whet it, which is where a colourful and attractive garnish can come in useful.

Whether – and when – you serve cheese is up to you. The English tradition is to serve it last, after the dessert, and this is said to be very good for the teeth. The French habit, on the other

hand, which English people are following increasingly, is to serve it before the dessert. This is a particularly good idea if you are serving red wine with your main course, and would like to move on to a sweet white wine to drink with the dessert.

The dessert course offers an enormous range of possibilities, but choose it with the preceding courses in mind and try to find something that contrasts well with them. Many desserts can be prepared in advance and can be left in the refrigerator, ready to be served whenever your guests are ready.

Planning a Menu

Most people find that planning the menu for a party is terrific fun and it certainly allows you to use all your creativity and ingenuity. The dishes you choose will depend on what type of party you are throwing – for example, whether it is a dinner party or a buffet, the time of year and the tastes of your guests. Unless it is a very special occasion, it is a good idea to limit the number of courses to three – or four, perhaps, if you are serving cheese – with coffee to finish. Choose one really spectacular course to impress everyone, and keep the rest simple. For a drinks and nibbles party choose six to eight different dishes, and when planning a barbecue, choose three or four main courses and serve them with bread and a variety of salads, followed by a simple cold dessert.

A Question of Balance

The most important thing when you are planning a menu is to aim for overall variety and balance. Variety is self-explanatory, but what exactly does balance mean? Well, what it means, above all, is not serving too much of any one thing and being careful about the overall spread of different ingredients, flavours, colours, temperatures, textures and even shapes.

Try, for example, not to serve every course hot. If there are to be three courses, say, as is

usually the case, it is probably best to serve one hot course and two cold ones. The hot dish generally takes the heart of the meal, especially during the winter months, though in summer this need not be the case. Then you might like to ring the changes by providing your guests with a surprise – you might serve the first and dessert courses hot, for example, and the main course cold, which would is not only unusual but also has the added advantage of being prepared in advance.

Similarly, it is usually better not to serve every course cold. One exception to this is where you are eating al fresco, in which case, cold food throughout the meal might seem to be more summery and therefore more appropriate.

There's absolutely nothing wrong, either, with mixing hot and cold in the same course. Serve a hot main dish with a cold dressed salad instead of hot vegetables, for example, or serve a cold salmon, say, with hot new potatoes. And combining hot and cold within the same dish can also be interesting: serve ice cream with hot chocolate sauce, perhaps, or make a warm salad with hot bacon or chicken livers. These are all things that can add an interesting surprise element to your meal.

Be alert, too, that the meal you are serving contains a variety of both colours and textures. Don't choose a menu consisting of a succession of all brown dishes – or all bright orange ones, or all beige – from beginning to end.

Do not serve two runny dishes in the same meal. Don't for example, serve soup, followed by another fairly liquid main course, such as a casserole. Similarly, don't serve a creamy soup if you are planning to offer a creamy dessert to finish. As a general rule, it's probably a good idea not to serve two courses that need to be eaten with a spoon.

Don't serve two complicated courses, both dominated by elaborate sauces. Make sure that at least one of them is a simple dish, which isn't 'messed about'.

Even the details are important. Just as you wouldn't serve lemon chicken followed by lemon mousse, so you shouldn't serve two dishes garnished with parsley, for example, or two buttery sauces, or two dishes sprinkled with

paprika or pine nuts or olives. Variety is the name of the game here and each course should both look and taste completely different.

Don't serve two pastry dishes in the same meal, even if the type of pastry is different. Don't, for example, serve chicken filo parcels as a starter and then follow these with a vegetable tart, and similarly don't serve steak and kidney pie, followed by apple tart.

All these suggestions may sound glaringly obvious and your indignation maybe deafening, but it is surprising how easy it is to forget and to do it without thinking, which is why it is so important to write down your proposed menu and to look at it carefully before you make any firm decisions and do your shopping. Sometimes things suddenly become more obvious when they are written down.

Similarly, try to avoid serving two hard, crunchy courses. Don't serve crudités to start with, which need such a lot of assiduous chewing, and a brittle meringue or nougat to finish.

Don't serve a fruity first course, such as melon or grapefruit if you are intending to finish the meal with a fresh fruit salad. There's nothing wrong with fruit and both dishes can be excellent choices – but not at the same meal.

A lot of people believe that it is wrong to serve more than the one fishy course in a meal. Not everyone agrees with this principle, however, and some believe that – as long as your guests like fish, of course – there's nothing wrong with serving it twice. Fish is a healthy option and you can't really eat too much of it. Think about a light fish pâté to open with, for example, or a smoked fish or prawn starter, and then follow this with a bold, fleshy fish such as

grilled fresh tuna or roasted monkfish. Two fish courses are probably better, anyway, than two meat courses. It would not be a good idea, for example, to serve chicken saté and then follow this, say, with roast lamb.

The Cheeseboard

With a little thought and care, the cheese course can be one of the highlights of a meal. For some people, it can actually be even more important than the dessert and they look forward to it right from the beginning of the meal. If you are aware that one of your friends or relatives feels like this, make sure that you do indeed supply a cheeseboard or they will be very disappointed and the whole meal is likely to have been, in their opinion, a sorry affair.

There is a great choice of different cheeses available in this country, some of them home-produced and many others imported from all round the world. Always choose a supplier who has a good reputation, and try to make sure that the cheeses you buy are in prime condition. Avoid buying any cheese that looks either too dry or sweaty, or that has any blue mould visible on the surface (unless, of course, it's a blue cheese, in which case this is quite deliberate).

When you are planning what cheeses to buy for your cheeseboard, try to make sure that the flavours and textures are well balanced. Three cheeses are usually enough for a good selection, though you can obviously supply more if you like. An ideal cheeseboard would contain one hard cheese, such as a good mature Cheddar, which is probably one of the most popular British cheeses, ranging in taste from the very mild to a strong nutty flavour; one semi-soft cheese, such as a mild, washed-rind cheese like Pont l'Evêque, which has a rich creamy flavour; and one soft cheese such as a ripe Brie, or a Camembert, which is slightly stronger in flavour than Brie, or a goat's cheese. If you want to add a fourth cheese, a blue cheese such as Stilton, Gorgonzola or Roquefort would be a good choice, or you could opt for a semi-hard cheese like Caerphilly or Jarlsberg. But ultimately, whatever your preferences, your

choice will probably also depend on what looks good in the shop and what is ripe enough to eat on the day that you need it. Look at all the cheeses carefully in the shop. Many good shops will allow you to taste a little piece before you commit yourself, which may help you make your decision.

When choosing a soft cheese such as Brie or Camembert, it is best – if the shop will allow you – to press the top surface lightly with the fingertips. The cheese should bulge slightly and should yield a little but not run when the surface is pressed. It should have no signs of any chalkiness in the centre, which is a sign that it has not ripened sufficiently and is likely to remain in this condition and never get any better.

Ideally, cheese should be stored in a cool, draught-free area, such as a larder. Failing that, the refrigerator is the next best thing. It should be taken out of the refrigerator and unwrapped at least an hour before it is needed at the table, so that it has sufficient time to come to room temperature.

It is worth noting, too, that most cheeses freeze well. They should be well wrapped and labelled before you put them in the freezer. Hard cheeses such as Cheddar are likely to become a little crumbly during the freezing process, but their flavour is unlikely to be impaired. Do not freeze soft cheeses such as Brie and Camembert for longer than six months.

It is well worth taking the time to make a cheeseboard look good. Cheeses are attractive in their own right and, as they need air to circulate around them, it is best to serve any accompaniments separately. Serve the cheese on a flat basket or a wooden or marble board, perhaps decorated with a few fresh figs, grapes, celery sticks or some vine leaves.

Some people prefer to eat many cheeses on their own without any accompaniment, but it is a good idea to offer bread or biscuits for those who like them with their cheese. Good crusty bread is preferable, with perhaps a few plain crackers and oatcakes as an alternative. Some people like butter with their cheese, in which case an unsalted one is best as it doesn't interfere with the flavours of the cheeses.

RIGHT • *Get all your glasses ready in advance, and prepare a range of garnishes such as cherries and slices of lemon and orange, to decorate the drinks.*

Advance Preparation

If you can manage to prepare most of the food in advance, you should be able to give your undivided attention to your guests at the time when this is what really matters. There are several ways in which you can do this.

Most people have a freezer these days, and this can play an important part in spreading the load over several days. If you're contemplating a very complicated meal with several courses and you know that time is going to be tight on the day, it is useful if you can prepare some of the dishes in advance and put them in the freezer for a day or two. This is a particularly good idea with fancy desserts, which won't suffer in the slightest from their sojourn in the freezer. If you are a regular party giver, double up on your

RIGHT • Home-baked cookies tied in festive ribbons will look really special served with coffee.

it is not really any more complicated than preparing for a smaller party. The secret of success is simply a question of careful advance planning. Plan every detail and leave nothing to chance. Work out your time schedule with military precision, making it as accurate and detailed as possible, and then stick to it rigidly. In the early preparatory days, this not need be any more specific than things like, 'Three weeks ahead, bake and freeze the cake', or 'Two weeks ahead, cook and freeze the lasagne', and 'One week ahead, take the tablecloth to the laundry and wash the china'. Work your way through your list systematically and then, as the time for the party draws near, you will need to work out a much more detailed plan of action, listing every single task you have to do, including such things as arranging the flowers, laying the table, making the salad dressing, taking things out of the freezer to give them to time to thaw, lighting the oven, garnishing the starter or carving the meat.

And above all, don't forget to allow time, too, for yourself. There's no point in managing to serve the most glorious meal if your hair is a mess and you haven't had time to change. Taking a bath, dressing and making up your face are as important as anything else, if you are going to be a relaxed and happy hostess.

When the party is over and has been a success, you'll wonder what all the fuss was about. Put your schedule away carefully somewhere – it will come in useful again next time you give a party.

Plan a menu that enables you to do most of the cooking and presentation well in advance. Keep the need for last-minute preparation in the kitchen down to an absolute minimum, even if this means axeing some of your favourite dishes. You will be pleased you did.

favourite dishes and freeze two of these in advance to save time. The freezer is also a boon for dealing with party leftovers, but remember that you should not freeze anything that has already been frozen.

The modern-day habit of offering a salad instead of vegetables allows you to prepare this in advance – though you should remember not to dress it until the last minute. If you can serve a salad, this will be at least one dish that you don't have to slave over a hot stove to prepare at the last moment.

Timetables

If you are planning an ambitious meal with several complicated courses, you may want to go to the lengths of writing a full schedule of all the tasks that you need to do and what time you should do them: such as when to switch the oven on, what food to start cooking when, when to put on the vegetables, and when to take the dessert out of the freezer or the cheese out of the refrigerator. There are often so many tiny but all-important details to remember, when you've got so much on your mind, that it is almost impossible not to forget something. A list of everything you need to do and when will eliminate this possibility and reduce your anxiety.

Cooking for a Crowd

Catering for large numbers of people can be a daunting prospect and can send the unpractised host or hostess into a flat spin, but

Courgette and Dill Soup

Fish in Wine Sauce

Parsnip Duchesse Potatoes

Raspberry Meringue
Cheesecake

Medium dry white wine

Informal Supper for Friends

Goats' Cheese with Peppers
and Pine Nuts

Chicken with Sizzling Garlic

Mixed salad or green
vegetable

Ice-cream Cake

Light red wine

Menu Suggestions

There are, of course, endless combinations of dishes which would work well to form a memorable meal or buffet. Following are some ideas for the occasions suggested here. You may have to adjust the quantities, depending on how many guests you have, and you will have to decide on green vegetables, salads and other accompaniments to go with the main courses. Wines of course are up to you, but we have made some suggestions for cocktails and punches where they seemed particularly appropriate.

ABOVE • If you are ever in doubt about what to serve to vegetarian friends, try vegetable brochettes marinated with a glaze of Dijon mustard, chopped mixed herbs, garlic and honey.

Cook-Ahead Supper for Friends

Chilli Chips

Sizzling Beef

Steamed Rice

Chocolate Mousse

Medium red wine

Winter Celebration Meal

Chilli Bean and Pepper Soup

Glazed Baked Ham

Parsnip Duchesse Potatoes

Chestnut Roulade

Full-bodied red wine

Al Fresco Summer Lunch

Spinach and Ricotta Puffs

Goats' Cheese with Peppers
    and Pine Nuts

Spiced Chicken Wings

Mini Pissaladière

Ravanie

Caribbean Fruit Kebabs

Summer Cup

Special Occasion Dinner

Baked Garlic with Brie

Roast Fillet of Salmon

Raspberry Meringue
    Cheesecake

Kir Royale

After-work Supper

Antipasto Focaccia

Walnut and Gorgonzola
    Chicory

Chocolate and Raspberry
    Bombes

Screwdriver

Celebration Buffet

Chicken Saté

Cheese and Onion Tartlets

Seeded Cheese Sablés

Toasted Chilli Cashews

Grilled Radicchio and Fontina
    Bruschetta with Anchoïade

Caribbean Fruit Kebabs

Chocolate Cups

Cheeseboard

Fruit Punch/Buck's Fizz

Vegetarian Dinner Party

Polenta Triangles

Green Vegetables in Thai
Spiced Coconut Sauce

Rice or flat noodles

Profiteroles

Eastern Dinner

Potstickers

Sichuan Scallops

Sizzling Beef

Fragrant Rice

Ice-cream Cake

China Tea

Family Birthday Picnic

Savoury Vol-au-Vents

Mini Pissaladière

Asparagus, Parmesan and
Egg Flan

Honey Cakes

Fruit Punch

Mexican Dinner Party

Chilli Chips or Toasted Chilli
Cashews

Chilli Bean and Pepper Soup

Spicy Chicken Wings

Pumpkin Puddings

Tequila Sunrise or Margaritas

Sea World Party

Prawns with Plum Sauce

Sweetcorn Chowder

Salmon and Courgette
Brochettes

Raspberry Meringue
Cheesecake

Florida Skies

Midsummer Tea Party

Profiteroles

Marron Meringues

Chocolate Cups

Traditional Shortbread

Summer Cup or Honeysuckle
Cup

Twenties Cocktail Party

Root Vegetable Crisps

Russian Potatoes

Toasted Chilli Cashews

Crispy Ricotta Parels

Bellini

Kir Royale

Orange Blossom

Dry Martini

Oriental Buffet

Vietnamese Spring Rolls

Chicken Saté

Prawn and Corn Fritters

Crispy Lamb with Lettuce

Siamese Slammer

Thai Sunrise

Fund-raising Morning

Cheese and Onion Tartlets

Traditional Shortbread

Sweet Biscotti

Marshmallow Crescents

Coffee

Smart Summer Dinner

Courgette and Dill Soup

Peppered Tuna Steaks with Fennel, Red Onions and Sugar Snap Peas

Chocolate and Raspberry Bombes

Mint Julep

Sunday Drinks Party

Briks

Cream Cheese, Egg and Celery Dip

Cucumber and Mint Raita

Crispy Ricotta Parcels

Polenta Triangles

Spinach and Ricotta Puffs

Blue Moon

Daiquiri

Christmas Drinks and Canapés Party

Houmous

Spicy Palmiers

Savoury Samosas

Marron Meringues

Tropical Christmas Cake

Mulled Red Wine

Mulled White Wine

Buck's Fizz

Presentation

Food that looks wonderful creates expectations in people and is more likely to taste good, too. Presentation is therefore an important aspect of entertaining, and goes a long way towards making food enticing. Choose attractive plates and dishes in which to serve it – perhaps even going as far as to make an ice bowl for serving ice cream, fruit salad or any other chilled dessert. A simple decoration or garnish will always add a little extra something. Above all, choose a garnish that marries well with the food you have chosen.

Herbs
Most herbs have pretty leaves, particularly chervil, sage, dill, coriander and parsley. Sprinkle chopped fresh herbs generously over a dish, or garnish it with a sprig of whatever herb has been used to flavour it.

Flowers

Edible flowers or petals can be used to
decorate both sweet and savoury foods.
Chives, pot marigolds, primroses, violets and
nasturtiums all make pretty decorations as well
as flavourful salad ingredients. They can be
used either fresh, or frosted with egg white
and sugar.

Fruit

Many fruits are very pretty. Try raspberries, redcurrants, kumquats or sliced strawberries to decorate summer cakes and desserts, or kiwi fruits and physalis for a change.

Citrus fruits

Orange, lemon and lime slices or wedges can add colour to sweet and savoury dishes and drinks. Pared rind also makes a great decoration. Remove the rind with a parer or cut off pieces using a vegetable peeler and slice it into fine strips before using it.

Vegetables

Many dishes look good served on a bed of salad leaves. Choose rocket for its distinctive peppery flavour and its prettily shaped leaves, and lollo rosso for its interesting frilly leaves, tinged with red. Whole or sliced chillies and diced sweet peppers are also attractive. Courgette or carrot ribbons, made with a potato peeler, are an effective garnish.

Finger Food

Crispy Ricotta Parcels

Makes: **24**

Preparation time: 30 minutes

Cooking time: 8–10 minutes

Oven temperature: 220°C/425°F/Gas Mark 7

250 g/8 oz ricotta cheese
125 g/4 oz frozen spinach, chopped and
   squeezed dry
125 g/4 oz smoked ham, finely chopped
¼ teaspoon ground nutmeg
8 sheets filo pastry
75 g/3 oz butter, melted
pepper
cress, to garnish (optional)

1 Place the ricotta cheese in a bowl with the spinach, ham and nutmeg and add pepper to taste. Mix well.

2 Put the sheets of filo pastry on a plate and cover with a damp tea towel. Working with one sheet of pastry at a time, cut each sheet into three equal strips and brush well with butter. Place a teaspoon of the cheese mixture at one end of each strip. Fold over diagonally to enclose the filling in a triangle of pastry and continue folding to make a neat three-cornered parcel.

3 Brush the parcel with more butter and place on a baking sheet. Repeat with the remaining filling, pastry and butter, to make a total of 24 small parcels.

4 Bake the parcels in a preheated oven at 220°C/425°F/Gas Mark 7 for 8–10 minutes until golden brown. Serve hot garnished with cress, if liked.

Chilli Chips

Use as little or as much chilli powder as you like, to coat these oven-roasted potato chips.

Serves: **4–6**

Preparation time: 5 minutes

Cooking time: about 1 hour

Oven temperature: 220°C/425°F/Gas Mark 7

4 large baking potatoes
4–6 tablespoons olive oil
½ teaspoon salt
1–2 teaspoons chilli powder, to taste
salad leaves, to garnish
soured cream or mayonnaise, to serve

1 Cut each potato into 8 wedges and place in a large bowl. Add the oil, salt and chilli powder and toss until evenly coated.

2 Transfer the potatoes to a baking sheet and roast in a preheated oven at 220°C/425°F/Gas Mark 7 for 15 minutes. Turn them over and cook for a further 15 minutes. Turn once more and cook for a final 25–30 minutes until crisp and golden.

3 Cool slightly and serve with soured cream or mayonnaise, garnished with salad leaves.

Seeded Cheese Sablés

These crisp, savoury, cocktail biscuits can be cut into any shape and served hot or cold.

Makes: **about 30**

Preparation time: 15 minutes, plus chilling

Cooking time: 9–12 minutes

Oven temperature: 200°C/400°F/Gas Mark 6

125 g/4 oz plain flour
75 g/3 oz unsalted butter, cut into small pieces
1 tablespoon English mustard powder
pinch of cayenne pepper
pinch of salt
125 g/4 oz mature Cheddar cheese, finely grated
40–50 g/1½–2 oz Parmesan cheese, finely grated
2 tablespoons black mustard seeds
1 tablespoon poppy seeds

1 Work the flour, butter, mustard, cayenne and salt in a food processor until the mixture resembles fine breadcrumbs. Add the Cheddar and continue to process for a few seconds until the mixture begins to come together to make a soft dough. Turn on to a lightly floured surface and knead gently. Wrap in clingfilm and refrigerate for about 30 minutes.
2 Roll out the pastry on a lightly floured surface to about 3 mm/⅛ inch thick. Cut into circles with a 6 cm/2½ inch fluted pastry cutter. Knead the trimmings together, roll out and cut more circles.
3 Line 2 heavy baking sheets with nonstick baking paper and place the sablés on them. Sprinkle with Parmesan and dust with mustard and poppy seeds. Bake in a preheated oven at 200°C/400°F/Gas Mark 6 for 9–12 minutes until crisp and light golden. Transfer the sablés to a wire rack with a palette knife. Serve hot, or set aside to cool and store in an airtight container to serve later.

Polenta Triangles

These triangles of set polenta are sandwiched together with mozzarella and coated in bread-crumbs, then deep-fried until crisp.

Makes: **18**

Preparation time: 10 minutes, plus setting and chilling

Cooking time: 10 minutes, plus 1–2 minutes per batch

900 ml/1½ pints water
15 g/½ oz butter
½ teaspoon sea salt
75 g/3 oz quick cooking polenta
15 g/½ oz Parmesan cheese, grated
175 g/6 oz mozzarella cheese
18 large basil leaves
4 tablespoons seasoned flour
2 eggs, beaten
50 g/2 oz dried white breadcrumbs
vegetable oil, for deep-frying
pepper

1 Grease a 20 x 30 cm/8 x 12 inch tin. Bring the water to a rolling boil, add the butter and salt and then gradually whisk in the polenta in a steady stream. Simmer over a low heat for 5–6 minutes, stirring constantly until the mixture comes away from the sides of the pan. Stir in the Parmesan, season with pepper and pour into the prepared tin. Smooth the surface and set aside to cool.
2 Turn out the set polenta and trim to form two 15 cm/6 inch squares. Cut each into nine 5 cm/2 inch squares and then cut each square in half diagonally, to make 36 triangles in all.
3 Cut the mozzarella into thin slices and then into triangles, the same size as the polenta.
4 Place a triangular slice of mozzarella over half the polenta triangles, top with a basil leaf

and a second piece of polenta. Dip the polenta sandwiches in the seasoned flour, then into the beaten egg and finally into the breadcrumbs to coat well. Chill for 1 hour.

5 Heat 5 cm/2 inches vegetable oil in a deep saucepan until it reaches 180–190°C/350–375°F, or until a cube of bread browns in 30 seconds.

6 Deep-fry the triangles in batches for 1–2 minutes until crisp and golden. Drain on kitchen paper and keep warm in a hot oven while frying the rest. Serve hot.

Spicy Palmiers

Makes: **24**

Preparation time: 10 minutes

Cooking time: 15 minutes

Oven temperature: 200°C/400°F/Gas Mark 6

250 g/8 oz puff pastry, thawed if frozen
2 tablespoons olive oil
½ teaspoon paprika pepper
pinch of cayenne pepper
3 tablespoons grated Parmesan cheese

1 Roll out the puff pastry thinly on a lightly floured surface and trim to make a 20 x 25 cm/8 x 10 inch rectangle.
2 Combine the oil, paprika, cayenne and Parmesan and brush three-quarters of the paste all over the pastry to give an even coating.
3 Fold in both long sides of pastry to meet in the middle, spread over a layer of the remaining paste and fold the pastry in half lengthways. Press down firmly.
4 Using a sharp knife cut the pastry into 24 thin slices and transfer, cut-side down, to 2 greased baking sheets.
5 Bake the pastries in a preheated oven at 200°C/400°F/Gas Mark 6 for 10 minutes, then turn them over and bake for a further 4–5 minutes until they are crisp and golden. Cool on a wire rack. These pastries are best eaten the day they are cooked.

Root Vegetable Crisps

These trendy crisps are easy to make at home, which means of course that you can use your favourite root vegetables.

Serves: **4–6**

Preparation time: 10 minutes

Cooking time: 8–10 minutes

2 beetroots
1 large potato
1 small sweet potato
2 carrots
2 parsnips
vegetable oil, for deep-frying
sea salt
cayenne pepper (optional)

1 Slice the vegetables into fine wafers using a potato peeler or mandoline, keeping them in separate batches. (It is best to cut the carrots and parsnips lengthways.)
2 Heat 5 cm/2 inches of vegetable oil in a deep saucepan until it reaches 180–190°C/350–375°F, or until a cube of bread browns in 30 seconds. Pat the vegetables dry on kitchen paper.
3 Again, keeping the vegetables separate, deep-fry them in batches for 30 seconds to 1½ minutes, until crisp and golden. Drain on kitchen paper and leave to cool on a wire rack.
4 Put the crisps into a large bowl and sprinkle with sea salt and a little cayenne, if using.

Prawn and Corn Fritters

Serves: **4**

Preparation time: 5 minutes

Cooking time: 10 minutes

20 g/¾ oz self-raising flour
65 g/2½ oz large raw prawns, minced
1 teaspoon Thai red curry paste
50 g/2 oz corn kernels
1 egg white
1 lime leaf, shredded
oil, for deep-frying
coriander sprigs, to garnish (optional)
hot sweet sauce, to serve

1 Put the flour, minced prawns, red curry paste, corn kernels, egg white and lime leaf in a bowl and mix thoroughly.
2 Heat the oil in a wok over a moderate heat, then put 1 heaped tablespoon of the mixture at a time into the hot oil. You may want to do this in 2 batches. Cook until golden brown – about 5 minutes.
3 Remove the fritters from the wok and drain on kitchen paper, then turn them on to a serving dish.
4 Garnish with coriander, if using, and serve with a hot sweet sauce.

Toasted Chilli Cashews

Makes: **about 250 g/8 oz**

Preparation time: 2 minutes

Cooking time: 2 minutes

1 tablespoon groundnut oil
1 garlic clove, finely chopped
250 g/8 oz roasted cashews
¼ teaspoon crushed dried chillies
1 spring onion, finely chopped
2 small fresh chillies (different colours),
  finely chopped
salt

1 Heat the oil in a wok and fry the garlic until golden brown. Remove and discard.
2 Add the cashews to the oil and sprinkle the crushed dried chillies over them. Stir-fry for 1 minute, then add the spring onion, chopped fresh chillies and salt to taste. Serve warm.

Grilled Radicchio and Fontina Bruschetta with Anchoïade

Serves: **4**

Preparation time: 10 minutes

Cooking time: 5 minutes

1 small radicchio head
125 g/4 oz Fontina cheese, rind removed
2–3 tablespoons olive oil
4 slices rustic Italian bread, preferably a day old
1 garlic clove, peeled but left whole
4 tablespoons Anchoïade
salt and pepper
Parmesan cheese shavings, to serve

1 Trim the radicchio leaves. Cut the heads lengthways into quarters, wash and leave to dry. Cut the Fontina into thin slices and slip them in between the leaves of the radicchio.
2 Heat half the oil in a large frying pan, add the radicchio and fry gently for 2–3 minutes. Turn carefully and cook for a further 2 minutes until the radicchio is golden and the cheese is melted.
3 Meanwhile, grill or toast the bread on both sides and rub all over with the garlic clove. Drizzle with a little extra oil and spread each slice with anchoïade. Season with salt and pepper to taste.
4 Top each bruschetta with the radicchio, scatter over the Parmesan then serve at once.

Anchoïade

Makes: **about 150 ml/¼ pint**

Preparation time: 5 minutes, plus soaking

125 g/4 oz canned anchovies in oil, drained
150 ml/¼ pint milk
25 g/1 oz pine nuts, toasted
2 garlic cloves, crushed
2 tablespoons chopped basil
1 tablespoon lemon juice
¼ teaspoon cayenne pepper
2 tablespoons olive oil
pepper

1 Put the anchovy fillets into a bowl, pour over the milk and set aside to soak for 10 minutes. Drain and pat dry.
2 Chop the anchovies. Put them into a blender or food processor with all the remaining ingredients except the oil. Work until smooth.
3 Transfer the paste to a bowl, stir in the oil and season to taste with pepper. The anchoïade can be stored in a screw-top jar in the refrigerator for up to 1 week.

Potstickers

These little dumplings take their name from the fact that they stick to the pan during cooking. Wonton wrappers, sometimes labelled dumpling pastries, are sold in small plastic packets. You can buy both round and square wrappers, but for this recipe you need the round ones, which are about 7.5 cm/3 inches in diameter. The wonton pastry is first fried, then cooked in stock.

Makes: **12–16**

Preparation time: about 30 minutes, plus chilling

Cooking time: about 25 minutes

12–16 round wonton wrappers
2 tablespoons groundnut oil
400 ml/14 fl oz hot chicken stock
soy sauce and/or chilli sauce, to serve

FILLING

8 large raw prawns, peeled
2 spring onions, quartered crossways
1 garlic clove, halved
2.5 cm/1 inch piece of fresh root ginger, peeled and sliced
1 teaspoon light soy sauce
½ teaspoon rice wine vinegar
pinch of sugar
salt and pepper

1 First make the filling. Put all the ingredients in a food processor, add a pinch of salt and pepper and work until finely minced. Turn the mixture into a bowl, cover and chill in the refrigerator for about 30 minutes until firm.

2 Place the wonton wrappers on a work surface. Heap about ½ teaspoon of the filling on each wrapper, placing it slightly off centre. Brush all around the edges of the wrappers with water. Fold the plain side of each wrapper over the mound of filling, making three pleats in it as you go. Press the rounded edges to seal in the filling, then pleat all around the rounded edges to make an attractive crimped finish. There is enough filling to make 12 quite plump dumplings or 16 less plump dumplings.

3 Heat 1 tablespoon of the oil in a wok until hot. Place half of the potstickers flat-side down in the hot oil and fry without disturbing for about 2 minutes until browned on the underside. Pour in half of the stock; this should be enough to just cover the potstickers. Bring to the boil, then lower the heat and simmer for about 10 minutes until the stock has been absorbed into the potstickers. Repeat with the remaining oil, potstickers and stock. Serve hot, with soy sauce and chilli sauce for dipping.

Briks

Briks (pronounced breeks) are turnovers from North Africa. Traditionally they are deep-fried and must be served immediately they are cooked otherwise they become heavy and greasy, but they can be baked, as in this recipe.

Makes: **about 24**

Preparation time: 30 minutes

Cooking time: 20 minutes

Oven temperature: 190°C/375°F/Gas Mark 5

about 250 g/8 oz filo pastry, thawed if frozen
olive oil, for brushing
sesame seeds, for sprinkling
FILLING
50 g/2 oz olives, pitted
3 anchovy fillets
3 sun-dried tomatoes in oil, drained and
  chopped
2 tablespoons chopped almonds
2 tablespoons chopped mixed coriander and
  parsley
3 soft-boiled eggs, chopped
squeeze of lemon juice, to taste
pepper

1 To make the filling, finely chop the olives and anchovy fillets then mix them with the tomatoes, almonds, coriander and parsley, eggs and lemon juice and season with pepper.
2 Cut the pastry into 10 x 25 cm/4 x 10 inch strips. Work with 3 or 4 strips at a time, keeping the remaining pastry covered with a damp tea towel.

3 Brush the strips lightly with oil and put a heaped teaspoon of the filling at the top right-hand corner of each one. Fold the corner down to make a triangle. Continue folding the triangle along the length of the strip. Place on a baking sheet and brush with oil. Repeat until all the filling has been used.
4 Sprinkle the briks with sesame seeds and bake in a preheated oven at 190°C/375°F/Gas Mark 5 for about 20 minutes until crisp and golden. Serve hot or warm.

Savoury Samosas

Makes: **about 16**

Preparation time: 25 minutes

Cooking time: 10 minutes

6 sheets filo pastry
oil, for deep-frying
Sweet and Sour Aubergine Relish
  (see page 186), to serve
FILLING ONE
250 g/8 oz new potatoes, cooked and cubed
50 g/2 oz young spinach, cooked
1 spring onion, finely sliced
FILLING TWO
175 g/6 oz cooked chicken, diced
1 leek, sliced and softened
salt and pepper

1 Stir together the ingredients for the two fillings and season well to taste.
2 Lay the filo sheets on a work surface and cut them into 10 cm/4 inch wide strips. Spoon a little of the filling in the corner of each strip and fold the pastry over to form a triangle, then do this twice more. Seal with a little water, pressing well together. Trim the pastry and continue making samosas, using both fillings.
3 Heat the oil in a deep saucepan and cook the samosas, in batches, for 2–3 minutes each. Drain on kitchen paper.
4 Serve the samosas warm with the relish.

Sweet and Sour Aubergine Relish

This tangy relish is excellent with Savoury Samosas (see page 184). It will keep for about 1 week in the refrigerator.

Serves: **8–10**

Preparation time: 10 minutes, plus cooling

Cooking time: about 45 minutes

150 ml/¼ pint sunflower oil
1 large onion, halved and thinly sliced
3 garlic cloves, crushed
1 kg/2 lb firm aubergines, cut into 1 cm/½ inch dice
6 tablespoons lemon juice
3–4 tablespoons demerara sugar
1 teaspoon ground cumin
¼ teaspoon cayenne pepper
salt

1 Heat 2 tablespoons of the oil and fry the onion and garlic until soft and beginning to colour. Using a slotted spoon, transfer to a large saucepan.

2 Heat one-third of the remaining oil until very hot and fry one-third of the aubergines very quickly until browned on all sides. Using the slotted spoon, transfer them to the pan with the onion. Repeat with the remaining oil and aubergines.

3 Stir the lemon juice, sugar, cumin and cayenne into the fried aubergine and onion mixture and season with salt to taste. Return to the heat and cover closely with a circle of greaseproof paper and the saucepan lid. Cook gently, stirring occasionally, for about 20 minutes until the mixture is thick and pulpy but still with texture.

4 Transfer to a bowl and leave to cool. Cover and refrigerate until required. Serve at room temperature.

Cream Cheese, Egg and Celery Dip

Serves: **8**

Preparation time: 10 minutes

200 g/7 oz cream cheese
300 ml/½ pint soured cream
4 hard-boiled eggs, shelled
2 tablespoons snipped chives
salt and pepper
1 celery head, to serve

1 Beat the cream cheese in a bowl until softened and smooth. Gradually mix in the soured cream.

2 Cut the eggs in half and scoop out the egg yolks. Set the yolks aside. Finely chop the egg whites and add to the cream cheese mixture with the chives and salt and pepper to taste.

3 Spoon the dip into a small bowl. Sieve the egg yolk over the top. Serve with celery, cut into dipping sticks.

Cucumber and Mint Raita

A mild-flavoured Indian yogurt dish which makes a lovely refreshing dip. If you like, add a little chopped fresh chilli or mint sauce, or some chopped coriander.

Serves: **4–6**

Preparation time: 5 minutes, plus chilling

200 ml/7 fl oz natural yogurt
7 cm/3 inch piece of cucumber, peeled and
    coarsely grated or chopped
2 tablespoons chopped mint
pinch of ground cinnamon
squeeze of lemon or lime juice
pepper
mint sprigs, to garnish

Put the yogurt into a bowl and beat lightly with a fork or whisk until smooth. Add the remaining ingredients and stir to combine. Cover and refrigerate until required. Serve chilled, garnished with mint sprigs.

Ginger and Lime Pickle Mayonnaise

You can vary the strength of this mayonnaise as you wish. Lime pickle can be very powerful whereas mango chutney is pleasantly mellow.

Makes: **300 ml/½ pint**

Preparation time: 30 minutes

1 lime
1 large egg yolk
¼ teaspoon English mustard powder
150 ml/¼ pint sunflower oil
4 tablespoons lime pickle or mango chutney
1 piece stem ginger preserved in syrup, cut into
    slivers
1 tablespoon finely chopped coriander
salt and pepper

1 Using a vegetable peeler, remove the rind from the lime in very thin strips, leaving the white pith attached to the flesh. Cut the rind into julienne strips. Remove the pith from the lime with a serrated knife and cut the flesh into segments.
2 To make the mayonnaise, put the egg yolk and mustard in a bowl, then add the oil, drop by drop, beating continually with a hand or electric whisk. After about 25 ml/1 fl oz oil has been incorporated, add the rest in a fine stream, still beating continually.

3 Squeeze the juice from half of the lime segments into the mayonnaise, then stir in the remaining lime segments and half the lime julienne, the pickle or chutney, ginger and coriander. Season as necessary, garnish with the remaining lime julienne, then cover and refrigerate until required.

Chilli Bean Dip

Houmous

This spicy dip is excellent with crudités, corn chips or fingers of warm or toasted pitta bread. It is also good spread on bruschetta and crostini, like a pâté.

Serves: **4**

Preparation time: 15 minutes

Cooking time: 30 minutes

Oven temperature: 240°C/475°F/Gas Mark 9

2 large red peppers
2 tablespoons olive oil
2 garlic cloves, crushed
1 small red chilli, deseeded and finely chopped
400 g/13 oz can red kidney beans, drained
½ teaspoon paprika
few drops of Tabasco sauce (if required)
salt and pepper
2 tablespoons snipped chives, to garnish

1 Halve the peppers lengthways and deseed. Lightly brush them inside and out with a little oil. Place on a lightly oiled baking sheet and roast in a preheated oven at 240°C/475°F/Gas Mark 9 for 15 minutes. Turn the peppers over and continue to roast until the edges begin to blacken and the flesh and skin begin to crumple. This will probably take another 15 minutes. Remove the peppers from the oven and leave until cool enough to handle, then peel off the skins.

2 Work the red pepper flesh, garlic and chilli in a food processor or blender until well chopped. Add the beans and paprika and continue to process until a coarse purée forms. This won't take long. Season with Tabasco, if using, and salt and pepper. With the machine running, add the rest of the oil to make a thick paste.

3 Pile the bean purée into a bowl and sprinkle with the chives. Cover and refrigerate until ready to serve.

Serves: **6**

Preparation time: 10–15 minutes, plus chilling

Cooking time: 1–1½ hours

250 g/8 oz chickpeas, soaked overnight and drained
2–3 garlic cloves
250 ml/8 fl oz lemon juice
5 tablespoons tahini paste
salt
TO SERVE
olive oil
Kalamata olives
cheese straws or biscuits

1 Place the chickpeas in a large saucepan of boiling water and cook for 1–1½ hours until soft. Drain and reserve the cooking liquid. Purée the chickpeas in a liquidizer or food processor with a little of the cooking liquid, then press the purée through a sieve to remove the skins.

2 Crush the garlic with a little salt and beat into the chickpea purée. Stir in alternate spoonfuls of the lemon juice and tahini, tasting as you go to adjust the flavour. Add more of the cooking liquid if needed to make a soft, creamy consistency. Taste, and adjust the seasoning if necessary. Spoon into a shallow serving dish and chill in the refrigerator for several hours.

3 Remove the houmous from the refrigerator about 10 minutes before serving. Create swirls on the surface with the back of a spoon, then drizzle with olive oil and garnish with olives. Serve with cheese straws or biscuits, to dip.

Traditional Shortbread

Serves: **6–8**

Preparation time: 15 minutes, plus chilling

Cooking time: 45 minutes–1 hour

Oven temperature: 150°C/300°F/Gas Mark 2

250 g/8 oz plain flour
125 g/4 oz ground rice
125 g/4 oz caster sugar, plus extra for dusting
pinch of salt
250 g/8 oz unsalted butter

1 Sift the plain flour, ground rice, sugar and salt into a mixing bowl. Soften the butter slightly, cut it up, and rub it into the dry ingredients with your fingers. When the mixture starts to bind, gather it together with one hand into a ball. Knead it on a lightly floured surface to a soft, smooth and pliable dough.

2 Place a 20 cm/8 inch flan ring on a greased baking sheet and put in the dough, pressing it out evenly with your knuckles to fit the ring. With the back of a knife, mark the shortbread into triangles. Prick right through to the baking sheet with a fork in a neat pattern. Cover the shortbread and chill for at least 1 hour before baking, to firm it up.

3 Bake the shortbread in a preheated oven at 150°C/300°F/Gas Mark 2 for 45 minutes–1 hour,

or until it is a pale biscuit colour but still soft. Remove the shortbread from the oven and leave to cool and shrink before lifting off the ring, then dust lightly with caster sugar. When cold, cut it into triangles and store in an airtight container until required.

Marshmallow Crescents

Makes: **25**

Preparation time: 30 minutes, plus chilling

Cooking time: 20 minutes

Oven temperature: 180°C/350°F/Gas Mark 4

175 g/6 oz white marshmallows
100 g/3½ oz butter, softened
1 egg
1 tablespoon vanilla sugar
generous pinch of salt
300 g/10 oz plain flour
½ teaspoon baking powder
50 g/2 oz plain chocolate, broken into pieces

1 Beat the marshmallows in a mixing bowl with the softened butter until pale and creamy. Add the egg, vanilla sugar and salt and mix well. Sift the flour with the baking powder and gradually stir it into the marshmallow mixture. Form into a ball, wrap in foil and chill in the refrigerator until firm, about 20 minutes.

2 Cut the dough into 4 pieces and roll each one into a long thin strip. Cut the strips into 10 cm/4 inch lengths and form into small crescents. Arrange the crescents on a baking sheet and bake in a preheated oven at 180°C/350°F/Gas Mark 4 for 10–15 minutes, until golden.

3 Carefully remove the crescents from the baking sheet with a palette knife and leave

them to cool on a wire rack. Put the chocolate into a heatproof bowl and melt it over a pan of hot water. Dip the tips of the crescents into the chocolate then allow the chocolate to dry thoroughly.

Fork Food

Spiced Chicken Wings

Serves: **4**

Preparation time: 10 minutes, plus marinating

Cooking time: 8–10 minutes

8 large chicken wings
flat leaf parsley sprig, to garnish
lime wedges, to serve
MARINADE
1 garlic clove
5 cm/2 inch piece of fresh root ginger,
  peeled and chopped
juice and finely grated rind of 2 limes
2 tablespoons light soy sauce
2 tablespoons groundnut oil
2 teaspoons ground cinnamon
1 teaspoon ground turmeric
2 tablespoons clear honey
salt
YELLOW PEPPER DIP
2 yellow peppers
2 tablespoons plain yogurt
1 tablespoon dark soy sauce
1 tablespoon chopped coriander
pepper

1 Place the marinade ingredients in a blender or food processor and blend until smooth.
2 Place the chicken in a bowl and pour over the marinade. Toss, cover and leave to marinate for 1–2 hours.
3 To make the dip, put the peppers under a preheated grill for 10 minutes, turning occasionally until they are charred and blistered. Put them into a plastic bag until cool, then peel off the skin and remove the seeds and white membrane. Put the flesh into a food processor or blender with the yogurt and blend until smooth. Pour into a bowl, season with soy sauce and pepper to taste and stir in the coriander. Cover and chill until needed.
4 Remove the chicken from the marinade and cook under a preheated grill or on a barbecue grill for 4–5 minutes on each side, basting with the remaining marinade. Garnish with a flat leaf parsley sprig, then serve with the dip and some lime wedges.

Russian Potatoes

Makes: **48**

Preparation time: 15 minutes

Cooking time: 20 minutes

24 baby new potatoes, scrubbed
150 ml/¼ pint Greek yogurt
50 g/2 oz black lumpfish roe
50 g/2 oz red lumpfish roe
salt
chopped dill, to garnish

1 Put the potatoes into a saucepan, cover with water and add a little salt. Bring to the boil, then simmer for about 20 minutes, or until just cooked. Drain and cool. Cut the potatoes in half, trimming a little skin from the bottoms if necessary so they sit flat.
2 Using a small knife, scoop out a cone of potato. Fill the hole with a little yogurt topped with a little lumpfish roe and garnish with dill.

Prawns with Plum Sauce

Serves: **8**

Preparation time: 10 minutes

4 tablespoons Chinese plum sauce
150 ml/¼ pint garlic mayonnaise
16 cooked tiger prawns, shelled but tails left on
spring onion curls, to serve

1 Stir together the plum sauce and mayonnaise until evenly coloured and smooth. Turn into a serving bowl.
2 Serve the dip with the prawns and spring onion curls.

Antipasto Focaccia

Serves: **10**

Preparation time: 20 minutes, plus standing

Cooking time: 25 minutes

Oven temperature: 230°C/450°F/Gas Mark 8

275 g/9 oz packet white bread mix
200 ml/7 fl oz warm water
200 g/7 oz mozzarella, grated
100 g/3½ oz salami, sliced
4 sun-dried tomatoes, chopped
8 oregano sprigs
2 teaspoons black pepper
2 tablespoons extra virgin olive oil

1 Lightly oil a 19 x 28 cm/7½ x 11 inch shallow tin. Make up the bread mix according to the packet instructions. Knead for 5 minutes.
2 Divide the dough in half and roll out to fit the base of the tin. Sprinkle with one-third of the grated mozzarella, followed by half of the salami. Top with half the remaining mozzarella, then the remaining salami.
3 Roll out the remaining dough to fit the tin. Set it on top of the salami, pressing the edges down well to seal. Sprinkle with the remaining cheese, the sun-dried tomatoes, oregano sprigs and pepper. Drizzle with oil. Cover loosely with clingfilm and leave to rise in a warm place for 40 minutes.
4 Bake in a preheated oven at 230°C/450°F/Gas Mark 8 for 25 minutes or until golden. Leave to cool for 5 minutes before cutting into slices.

Spinach and Ricotta Puffs

Makes: **48**

Preparation time: 20 minutes

Cooking time: 30 minutes

Oven temperature: 190°C/375°F/Gas Mark 5

500 g/1 lb shortcrust pastry
25 g/1 oz butter
125 g/4 oz spinach, chopped
large pinch grated nutmeg
125 g/4 oz ricotta cheese
2 egg yolks
75 ml/3 fl oz double cream
black pepper

1 Roll out the pastry on a lightly floured work surface. Using a 6 cm/2½ inch fluted cutter, cut out 48 rounds, re-rolling the trimmings as necessary. Line 48 patty tins with the pastry and prick the bases. Line with foil, fill with baking beans and bake in a preheated oven at 190°C/375°F/Gas Mark 5 for 10 minutes. Remove the foil and beans and bake for a further 5 minutes. Leave the oven on.
2 Meanwhile, melt the butter in a saucepan, add the spinach and cook until it begins to wilt. Remove the spinach from the heat, drain in a colander and season with nutmeg. Beat into the ricotta cheese with the egg yolks, cream and pepper.
3 Arrange the baked pastry cases on baking sheets and spoon in the mixture. Bake in the oven for 15 minutes.

Savoury Vol-au-vents

Makes: **24**

Preparation time: 30 minutes

Cooking time: 15 minutes

24 ready-made puff pastry vol-au-vents
chopped herbs, to garnish
PEPPER FILLING
½ x 275 g/9 oz jar antipasto peppers
15 black pitted olives, chopped
2 tablespoons chopped oregano
MUSHROOM FILLING
375 g/12 oz wild mushrooms
25 g/1 oz butter
2 garlic cloves, finely chopped
6 tablespoons double cream
MASCARPONE AND GRAPE FILLING
250 g/8 oz mascarpone cheese
175 g/6 oz seedless grapes, halved
salt and pepper

1 Cook the vol-au-vents according to
the packet instructions. Leave to cool on
wire racks.
2 To make the pepper filling, stir together
the peppers, olives and oregano.
3 To make the mushroom filling, slice the
mushrooms as necessary. Melt the butter in a
saucepan, add the mushrooms and garlic and
cook for 5 minutes. Stir in the cream, bring to
the boil then simmer for about 3 minutes or
until thickened.
4 To make the mascarpone and grape filling,
beat the mascarpone until soft, fold in the
grape halves and season with salt and pepper.
5 Spoon the fillings into the vol-au-vent cases
and garnish with chopped herbs.

Walnut and Gorgonzola Chicory

Serves: **8–10**

Preparation time: 15 minutes

2 heads chicory
125 g/4 oz Gorgonzola cheese, cubed
50 g/2 oz walnuts, coarsely chopped
4 tablespoons crème fraîche
flat leaf parsley, to garnish

1 Take the leaves from the chicory stalk,
discarding any blemished leaves.
2 Stir together the Gorgonzola, walnuts and
crème fraîche.
3 Spoon the Gorgonzola mixture into the
chicory leaves. Arrange on a serving platter
and garnish with flat leaf parsley.

Mini Pissaladière

This classic Provençal tart can be made with pizza dough as the base or with a pastry case. The topping however is always the same – onions, anchovies and olives.

Serves: **6**

Preparation time: 20 minutes, plus chilling

Cooking time: 50 minutes

Oven temperature: 200°C/400°F/Gas Mark 6

4 tablespoons olive oil
1 kg/2 lb onions, thinly sliced
2 garlic cloves, crushed
2 teaspoons chopped thyme
1 teaspoon salt
1 teaspoon sugar
3 anchovy fillets, halved lengthways
6 stuffed green olives
3 tablespoons grated Parmesan cheese
salad leaves, to garnish
lemon wedges, to serve
PASTRY
125 g/4 oz plain flour
½ teaspoon salt
50 g/2 oz butter
1–2 tablespoons iced water

1 To make the pastry, sift the flour and salt into a bowl and rub in the butter until the mixture resembles fine breadcrumbs. Work in enough iced water to form a soft dough. Knead lightly then chill for 30 minutes.
2 Heat the oil in a heavy-based frying pan and fry the onions, garlic, thyme, salt and sugar for about 25 minutes until golden and caramelized. Set aside to cool.
3 Divide the pastry into 6 pieces, roll out each piece on a lightly floured surface and use to line six 7 cm/3 inch tartlet tins. Prick the bases with a fork and chill for a further 20 minutes.
4 Line each pastry case foil with baking beans and bake blind in a preheated oven at 200°C/400°F/Gas Mark 6 for 15 minutes. Remove the foil and beans. Leave the oven on.
5 Divide the onion mixture between the pastry cases and garnish the tops with an anchovy cross and olive slices. Sprinkle over the Parmesan and bake for 10 minutes. Cool a little on a wire rack. Garnish with salad leaves and serve warm with lemon wedges.

Glazed Baked Ham

The soaking time for the gammon depends on how salty it is, so check with your supplier when you buy the joint. Soak overnight if in doubt

Serves: **10–15**

Preparation time: 5 minutes plus soaking and cooling

Cooking time: 2½–3½ hours

Oven temperature: 190°C/375°F/Gas Mark 5

2.5–4 kg/5–8 lb gammon joint, either on the
   bone, or boned and rolled
2 bay leaves
2 tablespoons demerara sugar
150 ml/¼ pint ginger ale
GLAZE
3 tablespoons ginger marmalade
6 tablespoons demerara sugar

1 Place the gammon in a large saucepan of cold water and leave to soak for 2–12 hours.
2 Drain the gammon, then weigh and calculate the cooking time at 25 minutes per 500 g/1 lb, plus 20 minutes. For a joint over 3 kg/6 lb allow 20 minutes per 500 g/1 lb, plus 20 minutes.
3 Return the gammon to the pan and pour in enough cold fresh water to cover. Add the bay leaves and sugar and bring to the boil. Cover, lower the heat and simmer for half the estimated cooking time.
4 Remove the gammon from the pan and strip off the skin. Stand the gammon on a large sheet of foil in a roasting tin and score the fat diagonally in a trellis pattern. Mix together the marmalade and sugar and spread over the surface of the fat.
5 Pour the ginger ale around the joint and enclose in foil, sealing the edges firmly. Cook in a preheated oven, 190°C/375°F/Gas Mark 5, for the remainder of the cooking time.
6 Baste the gammon with the ginger ale, rewrap with the foil and cook until 20 minutes before the end of the cooking time. Fold back the foil, baste again and return to the oven and leave the gammon to cool.

Vietnamese Spring Rolls

Makes: **40**

Preparation time: about 45 minutes, plus soaking

Cooking time: 40–50 minutes

50 g/2 oz thin cellophane (bean thread) noodles
15 g/½ oz dried black ear fungus
125 g/4 oz minced pork
2 shallots, chopped
3 garlic cloves, crushed
2.5 cm/1 inch piece of fresh root ginger, peeled and finely chopped
½ tablespoon soy sauce
10 round rice papers
2 eggs, beaten
pepper
groundnut oil, for deep-frying
mint sprig, to garnish
chilli sauce or Cucumber and Mint Raita (see page 188), to serve

1 Soak the noodles and fungus in separate bowls of warm water for 20 minutes, until soft.
2 Using scissors snip the noodles into 2.5 cm/1 inch lengths and chop the fungus into small pieces. Mix with the pork, shallots, garlic, ginger, soy sauce and pepper.
3 With the scissors cut each round of rice paper into 4 quarters. Brush each quarter with egg and leave to soften for a couple of minutes. Place 1 heaped teaspoon of filling towards the rounded edge of the rice paper, fold the sides in and roll up towards the pointed end. Repeat with the remaining filling and rice paper.
4 Heat the oil for deep-frying in a saucepan until a cube of bread browns in 2 minutes. Add about 6 spring rolls and cook for 6–8 minutes or until they are golden brown and the filling cooked through. Repeat with the remaining spring rolls. Garnish with a sprig of mint and serve with chilli sauce or the raita.

Chicken Saté

Soak the bamboo skewers in cold water for 30 minutes before use. This will prevent them from burning under the grill.

Makes: **8**

Preparation time: 20 minutes, plus marinating

Cooking time: 4–6 minutes

500 g/1 lb boneless, skinless chicken breast fillets
coriander sprigs, to garnish
lime wedges, to serve

MARINADE
1 small onion, finely chopped
2 teaspoons grated fresh root ginger
2 garlic cloves, crushed
2 tablespoons lime juice
1 tablespoon dark soy sauce
1 tablespoon garam masala
½ teaspoon salt
SATE SAUCE
1 tablespoon groundnut oil
1 garlic clove, crushed
4 tablespoons crunchy peanut butter
¼ teaspoon dried chilli flakes
1 tablespoon dark soy sauce
1 tablespoon lime juice
1 teaspoon clear honey
2 tablespoons coconut cream

1 Cut the chicken breasts on the diagonal into very thin strips and place in a shallow dish. Combine the marinade ingredients and pour over the chicken. Stir once, cover and leave to marinate overnight.
2 To make the saté sauce, heat the groundnut oil in a small pan and gently fry the garlic for 2–3 minutes until softened. Stir in all the remaining ingredients and heat gently until boiling. Pour into a serving dish.
3 Lift the chicken out of the marinade and pat dry. Thread the chicken on to 8 pre-soaked bamboo skewers, zig-zagging back and forwards as you go. Cook under a preheated grill for 2–3 minutes on each side until charred and cooked through. Garnish with coriander sprigs and serve with the saté sauce and lime wedges.

Cheese and Onion Tartlets

Makes: **20**

Preparation time: 15 minutes, plus chilling

Cooking time: 15 minutes

Oven temperature: 200°C/400°F/Gas Mark 6

250 g/8 oz shortcrust pastry
150 g/5 oz onion, finely chopped
6 tablespoons milk
150 g/5 oz mature Cheddar cheese, grated
125 g/4 oz Red Leicester cheese, grated
1 egg, beaten
salt and pepper

1 Roll out the pastry thinly on a lightly floured work surface and use to line about twenty 6 cm/1½ inch tartlet tins. Chill for 30 minutes.
2 Put the onion and milk into a saucepan. Bring to the boil, then simmer for 1 minute. Remove from the heat and stir in the cheeses, egg and salt and pepper. Leave to stand for 5 minutes.
3 Divide the mixture among the tartlets. Bake in a preheated oven at 200°C/400°F/Gas Mark 6 for 15 minutes until golden. Serve warm.

Asparagus, Parmesan and Egg Flan

Serves: **4**

Preparation time: 35 minutes, plus chilling

Cooking time: 40–45 minutes

Oven temperature: 200°C/400°F/Gas Mark 6, then 180°C/350°F/Gas Mark 4

PASTRY
175 g/6 oz plain flour
75 g/3 oz chilled butter, diced
FILLING
175 g/6 oz thin asparagus spears
5 eggs
150 ml/¼ pint single cream
25 g/1 oz Parmesan cheese, grated
salt and pepper

1 Measure the flour in a bowl, add the butter and rub in with the fingertips until the mixture resembles fine breadcrumbs. Add enough cold water, about 2 tablespoons, to mix to a firm dough. Roll out on a lightly floured surface and line a 20 cm/8 inch flan tin. Chill for 30 minutes, if time permits.
2 Fill the pastry case with crumpled foil and bake in a preheated oven at 200°C/400°F/Gas Mark 6 for 15 minutes, then remove the foil and return the pastry case to the oven for 10 minutes more. Lower the oven temperature to 180°C/350°F/Gas Mark 4.
3 Make the filling. Trim the woody ends from the asparagus. Stand them upright in a tall saucepan. Add salted water to cover all but the tips of the asparagus. Cover the pan with foil or a lid and cook for 7–10 minutes, until tender. Drain the asparagus in a colander and refresh under cold running water. Drain again.
4 Beat one of the eggs in a bowl with the cream. Add salt and pepper to taste. Arrange the asparagus in the base of the flan case. Break each of the remaining 4 eggs in turn into a saucer, and carefully slide them into the flan case. Pour over the cream mixture and sprinkle with the Parmesan.
6 Return the flan to the oven for a further 15–20 minutes, until the eggs have just set. Serve the flan warm.

sugar and orange rind and juice in a saucepan and stir over a gentle heat until the sugar has dissolved. Add the honey and boil gently for 3 minutes.

5 When the cake is ready, remove it from the oven and pierce it at evenly spaced intervals with a fine skewer. Spoon the syrup glaze evenly over the top. Sprinkle with the toasted sesame seeds. Leave to cool.

6 Cut into diamond shapes and serve. This cake keeps for up to 1 week, covered with foil, in a cool place.

Profiteroles

Serves: **8–10**

Preparation time: 20 minutes

Cooking time: 15–20 minutes

Oven temperature: 200°C/400°F/Gas Mark 6

65 g/2½ oz plain flour
150 ml/¼ pint water
50 g/2 oz butter, cut into pieces
pinch of salt
2 large eggs, beaten
250 ml/8 fl oz double cream
1 tablespoon strong cool coffee
MOCHA ICING
125 g/4 oz plain chocolate
1 tablespoon instant coffee dissolved in
  1½ tablespoons hot water
200 g/7 oz icing sugar, sifted

1 Lightly grease a baking sheet. Sift the flour on to a sheet of paper.
2 Put the water, butter and salt into a saucepan and bring to the boil over a moderate heat. Remove the pan from the heat, add the flour all at once and beat hard with a wooden spoon for about 20 seconds, until the mixture comes clear of the sides of the pan. Return the pan to a very low heat and beat for about 30 seconds.
3 Leave to cool slightly. Beat in the eggs, little by little, using just enough egg to make a glossy dough, which falls from the spoon.
4 Place 8–10 spoons of dough on the baking sheet. Bake in a preheated oven at 200°C/400°F/Gas Mark 6 for 20–25 minutes. Split each profiterole horizontally to let out the steam and leave to cool on a wire rack.
5 Combine the cream and coffee and whip until stiff. Use to fill the profiteroles.
6 To make the mocha icing, break the chocolate into a heatproof bowl and place over a saucepan of very hot water until melted. Remove from the heat and beat in the dissolved coffee, then the icing sugar. Use to decorate the tops of the profiteroles.

Tropical Christmas Cake

Serves 10

Preparation time: 30 minutes

Cooking time: 1½ hours

Oven temperature: 160°C/325°F/Gas Mark 3

300 g/10 oz unsalted butter
250 g/8 oz caster sugar
3 large eggs, beaten
375 g/12 oz self-raising flour, sifted
425 g/14 oz can pineapple rings, in syrup
75 g/3 oz glacé cherries, chopped
75 g/3 oz mixed peel, chopped
40 g/1½ oz angelica, chopped
50 g/2 oz walnuts, chopped
40 g/1½ oz desiccated coconut
125 g/4 oz sultanas
toasted coconut shavings, to decorate
COCONUT ICING
40 g/1½ oz unsalted butter
175 g/6 oz icing sugar
25 g/1 oz desiccated coconut

1 Grease and flour a 1.5 litre/2½ pint ring mould or a 20 cm/8 inch cake tin.
2 Put the butter and sugar in a mixing bowl and cream until soft and light. Gradually beat in the eggs. Fold the sifted flour and into the creamed mixture.
3 Drain the canned pineapple, setting aside 3 tablespoons of syrup for the icing and 7 tablespoons of syrup for the cake. Chop the pineapple rings finely. Fold the chopped pineapple, cherries, mixed peel, angelica and

walnuts into the cake mixture with the coconut, sultanas and the 7 tablespoons of pineapple syrup.

4 Put the mixture into the prepared ring mould or cake tin and bake in a preheated oven at 160°C/325°F/Gas Mark 3 for 1¼ hours if using a ring mould and 1½ hours if using a 20 cm/8 inch tin. Leave the cake to cool for at least 10 minutes in the tin, then unmould it carefully and leave to cool completely.

5 To make the icing, melt the butter in a saucepan and remove from the heat. Sift the icing sugar into the butter, then add the reserved pineapple syrup and the desiccated coconut and stir to combine. Spread the icing over the top of the cake and a little way down the sides. Scatter the toasted coconut shavings over the top of the cake.

Sit Down Meals

Sweetcorn Chowder

Chowder was originally a soupy stew from Brittany. It was taken to Newfoundland by the Breton fishermen, and then found its way south down the Atlantic coast to New England.

Serves: **6**

Preparation time: about 10 minutes

Cooking time: 45–55 minutes

50 g/2 oz butter
1 large onion, finely diced
3 garlic cloves, finely chopped
125 g/4 oz potato, finely diced
300 ml/½ pint milk
75 ml/3 fl oz medium sherry
600 ml/1 pint vegetable or chicken stock
750 g/1½ lb fresh or frozen sweetcorn kernels or
    2 x 325 g/11 oz cans sweetcorn kernels,
    drained
65 ml/2½ fl oz single cream
2 teaspoons lime juice
2 tablespoons finely snipped chives
salt and pepper
vegetable oil, for deep-frying
sage leaves, to garnish

1 Melt the butter in a large saucepan, add the onion and garlic and fry over a gentle heat without colouring until soft. Add the diced potato and cook for a few minutes. Add the milk, sherry and stock, season with salt and pepper and bring to the boil. Reduce the heat to a simmer and cook for 10–15 minutes.
2 Add the sweetcorn, return to the boil and simmer for 10–15 minutes. Meanwhile, prepare the sage garnish. Heat the oil in a deep-fryer to 220°C/425°F, drop in the sage leaves and deep-fry for 20–30 seconds until crisp. Drain on kitchen paper and keep warm.
3 When the soup is ready, pour three-quarters

of it into a food processor or blender and purée until smooth. Add the purée to the soup remaining in the pan and return to the boil.
4 Season with salt and pepper and stir in the cream and lime juice, adding a little extra stock if necessary to obtain the desired consistency. Heat the chowder thoroughly and stir in the chives. Serve immediately, garnished with the sage leaves.

Chilli Bean and Pepper Soup

Serves: **6**

Preparation time: about 20 minutes

Cooking time: about 50 minutes

2 tablespoons sunflower oil
1 large onion, finely chopped
4 garlic cloves, finely chopped
2 red peppers, cored, deseeded and diced
2 red chillies, deseeded and finely chopped
900 ml/1½ pints vegetable stock
750 ml/1¼ pints tomato juice or passata
1 tablespoon double concentrate tomato purée
1 tablespoon sun-dried tomato paste
2 tablespoons sweet chilli sauce, or more to
    taste
400 g/13 oz can red kidney beans, drained
2 tablespoons finely chopped coriander
AVOCADO SALSA
1 firm ripe avocado

2 tablespoons lime juice
1 tablespoon finely chopped coriander
2 spring onions, finely sliced
salt and pepper
TO GARNISH
coriander sprigs
tortilla chips

1 First make the avocado salsa. Cut the avocado in half, remove the stone and peel off the skin. Cut the flesh into 1 cm/½ inch dice and put them into a bowl with the lime juice, coriander and spring onions. Season to taste with salt and pepper and toss lightly to combine without breaking up the avocado. Cover and refrigerate until required.
2 Heat the oil in a large saucepan and fry the onion and garlic until soft but not coloured. Stir in the red peppers and chillies and fry for a few minutes. Stir in the stock and tomato juice or passata, the tomato purée and paste, chilli

sauce, kidney beans and coriander. Bring to the boil, cover and simmer for 30 minutes.
3 Cool slightly, then purée in a food processor or blender until smooth. Return the soup to the pan and taste and adjust the seasoning, adding a little extra chilli sauce if necessary. Bring to the boil and serve in warmed soup bowls, topped with avocado salsa and coriander sprigs and accompanied by tortilla chips.

Courgette and Dill Soup

A flavoursome soup, perfect in the height of summer when there is a glut of courgettes. It is excellent served chilled and freezes well. For an entirely different taste, use fresh basil leaves instead of dill.

Serves: **8**

Preparation time: 10–15 minutes

Cooking time: 30–40 minutes

2–3 tablespoons sunflower or light olive oil
1 large onion, chopped
2 garlic cloves, crushed
1 kg/2 lb courgettes, sliced or roughly chopped
1.2–1.5 litres/2–2½ pints vegetable or
  chicken stock
2–4 tablespoons finely chopped dill
salt and pepper
TO GARNISH
125 ml/4 fl oz single cream
dill fronds

1 Heat the oil in a large saucepan and gently fry the onion and garlic until soft but not coloured. Add the courgettes, cover tightly with greaseproof paper and cook over a low heat for 10–15 minutes until tender. Add the stock, cover with a lid and simmer for a further 10–15 minutes.

2 Using a slotted spoon, transfer the courgettes and a little of the stock to a food processor or blender. Purée until smooth, then pour into a clean saucepan. Add the remaining stock and the dill, season to taste with salt and pepper, then bring to the boil.

3 Serve in warmed soup bowls, garnished with a swirl of cream and fresh dill fronds.

Goats' Cheese with Peppers and Pine Nuts

Serves: **4**

Preparation time: 15 minutes

Cooking time: 10–15 minutes

Oven temperature: 200°C/400°F/Gas Mark 6

40 g/1½ oz pine nuts
15 g/½ oz fresh breadcrumbs, toasted
½ tablespoon finely chopped basil
1 small garlic clove, finely chopped
2 x 65 g/2½ oz crottins de Chavignol cheeses,
  halved

1 tablespoon pine nut or hazelnut oil
4 small roasted red peppers, skinned, deseeded
  and cut into thin strips
VINAIGRETTE
½ teaspoon Dijon mustard
1 small garlic clove, crushed
50 ml/2 fl oz extra virgin olive oil
1 teaspoon white wine vinegar
salt and pepper
TO GARNISH
12 small basil leaves
8 whole chives

1 Spread the pine nuts on a heavy baking sheet and toast under a preheated hot grill, tossing frequently until they are an even golden colour. Don't overbrown them or they will taste bitter.

2 Chop 15 g/½ oz of the toasted pine nuts and combine them with the breadcrumbs, chopped basil and garlic. Brush each piece of cheese lightly with oil, then coat them evenly in the nutty crumbs. Set on a lightly oiled baking sheet and bake in a preheated oven at 200°C/400°F/Gas Mark 6 for 8–10 minutes until the cheese is warmed through and beginning to melt at the edges.

3 Meanwhile, make the vinaigrette. Put all the ingredients into a screw-topped jar and shake vigorously to combine. Taste and adjust the seasoning if necessary.

4 Arrange the pepper slivers on 4 large serving plates. Carefully lift the cheese off the baking sheet and set on top of the peppers.

Shake the dressing and drizzle a little over each serving. Garnish with the reserved whole toasted pine nuts, the basil leaves and chives and serve immediately.

Salmon and Courgette Brochettes

These brochettes can also be made with fresh tuna or swordfish. Mashed potatoes flavoured with olive oil go very well with them. If you are using wooden skewers soak them in cold water for 30 minutes first so that they do not burn.

Serves: **4**

Preparation time: 15 minutes, plus marinating

Cooking time: about 5 minutes

750 g–1 kg/1½–2 lb salmon fillet, skinned and cut into 1 cm/½ inch cubes
375 g/12 oz courgettes, cut into 1 cm/½ inch pieces
MARINADE
8 tablespoons sunflower oil
2 tablespoons light sesame seed oil
2 tablespoons sesame seeds
1 garlic clove, crushed
1–2 tablespoons lime juice
pepper
TO SERVE
rocket
whole chives
lime wedges

1 First prepare the marinade. Put all the ingredients into a large bowl and whisk together. Add the salmon and courgette pieces and toss to coat them thoroughly. Cover the bowl and leave the salmon to marinate for about 30 minutes.

2 Thread the salmon and courgette pieces alternately on to the skewers and cook the brochettes under a preheated very hot grill or over a hot barbecue for about 5 minutes, turning them frequently and brushing with the marinade to keep the fish and courgettes from drying out. The fish is cooked when it is just beginning to look milky. Take care not to overcook it or it will become dry and tough. Serve immediately on a bed of rocket and garnish with whole chives and lime wedges.

Green Vegetables with Thai Spiced Coconut Sauce

Serves: **4**

Preparation time: 10–15 minutes

Cooking time: 30–40 minutes

175 g/6 oz mangetouts, topped and tailed and halved on the diagonal, if large

2 large courgettes, cut into 5 mm/¼ inch slices

125 g/4 oz shelled peas

250 g/8 oz broccoli florets, trimmed

red chilli rings, to garnish

COCONUT SAUCE

3 tablespoons vegetable oil

1 large onion, finely chopped

4 garlic cloves, finely chopped

3–4 teaspoons Thai green curry paste

2 teaspoons ground turmeric

2 teaspoons brown sugar

2 x 400 g/13 oz cans coconut milk

1 tablespoon lime juice

3 tablespoons desiccated coconut

175 ml/6 fl oz vegetable stock

1 tablespoon cornflour

50 ml/2 fl oz double cream

4 tablespoons chopped coriander

salt and pepper

1 First make the sauce. Heat the oil in a large saucepan and fry the onion and garlic until soft but not coloured. Stir in the curry paste, turmeric, sugar, coconut milk, lime juice, desiccated coconut and stock, mixing well to blend. Bring to the boil and cook quickly, stirring frequently, for 10–15 minutes to reduce the sauce slightly and concentrate the flavours.

2 Blend the cornflour with the cream to make a smooth paste, add to the sauce and cook for a few minutes to thicken, then stir in half of the coriander. Add the mangetout, courgettes and peas and simmer gently.

3 Steam the broccoli for 4 minutes, then add it to the sauce and cook for a few minutes until all the vegetables are tender. Season to taste, sprinkle with the remaining coriander and serve immediately, garnished with red chilli rings.

Tuna Teriyaki

Fish or beef teriyaki cooks to a wonderful golden red crust and is slightly crispy on the outside and deliciously juicy on the inside. For this Japanese recipe make sure the tuna is as fresh as possible and do not overcook it. Heating the pan until it is very hot is essential for sealing in the juices and creating a golden crust.

Serves: **4**

Preparation time: 20–30 minutes, plus marinating

Cooking time: about 5 minutes

750 g/1½ lb very fresh tuna, cut into 5 cm/2 inch squares or rectangles
½ teaspoon salt
2 tablespoons vegetable oil
TERIYAKI SAUCE
125 ml/4 fl oz Japanese rice wine
4 tablespoons dark soy sauce
2 teaspoons caster sugar
2 teaspoons roughly chopped fresh root ginger
TO SERVE
12 asparagus spears, blanched
pickled ginger

1 First make the teriyaki sauce. Put the rice wine, soy sauce and caster sugar in a small saucepan and bring to the boil. Remove from the heat and leave to cool. Press the ginger through a garlic press and stir the juice into the sauce.
2 Rub both sides of the fish with salt to firm it. Set aside for 30 minutes, then rinse off the salt and put the fish pieces in the teriyaki sauce and leave to marinate for 1 hour.
3 Heat the oil in a pan until smoking hot. Remove the tuna from the marinade and add to the hot oil. Sear the surface, turn the tuna

over and sear the second side and cook for a further 1 minute. Pour the teriyaki sauce over the fish and cook for 1 minute more.
4 Remove the fish from the pan and serve with asparagus spears. Allow the sauce to bubble and thicken and then spoon a little over each of the pieces of fish and serve with a mound of pickled ginger.

Sichuan Scallops

Food from the region of Sichuan, in west China, is hot and spicy. Chilli, ginger, onion and garlic are used liberally and are in great evidence in this fiery scallop dish. The scallop is a very tender piece of seafood and needs only to be shown to the heat of the wok, for an instant, in order to sear the outside. Never overcook.

Serves: **4**

Preparation time: 10–15 minutes

Cooking time: 5 minutes

2 tablespoons oil
750 g/1½ lb scallops
2 garlic cloves, crushed
1 dried red chilli, finely chopped
½ teaspoon Chinese five spice powder
2.5 cm/1 inch piece of fresh root ginger, peeled and finely shredded
2 tablespoons Chinese rice wine or dry sherry
2 tablespoons dark soy sauce
3 tablespoons water
6 spring onions, diagonally sliced
1 small onion, sliced
1 teaspoon caster sugar
2 shredded spring onions, to garnish

1 Heat the oil in a wok or heavy-based frying pan until smoking hot. Add the scallops and sear on both sides then remove and reserve.
2 Add the garlic, chilli, five spice powder and ginger and stir-fry for 1 minute. Add the remaining ingredients and cook for 1 minute then return the scallops to the wok and stir-fry them in the sauce for no longer than 2 minutes or they will become tough.
3 Arrange the scallops with their sauce on a dish and garnish with the spring onions.

Roast Fillet of Salmon

This is a wonderfully simple recipe for an elegant summer meal. It can be prepared in advance and takes just a few minutes to cook and assemble.

Serves: **4**

Preparation time: 20–30 minutes

Cooking time: 10–12 minutes

Oven temperature: 240°C/475°F/Gas Mark 9

½ tablespoon sunflower oil
4 x 150–175 g/5–6 oz pieces of salmon fillet,
  skin on but scaled
salt and pepper
basil leaves, to garnish
COMPOTE
4 ripe tomatoes, skinned, deseeded and cut into
  5 mm/¼ inch dice
1 large firm, ripe avocado, stoned, peeled and
  cut into 5 mm/¼ inch dice
1–2 tablespoons extra virgin olive oil
4–5 tablespoons lime juice
dash of Worcestershire sauce
dash of Tabasco sauce
FRESH BASIL DRESSING
150 ml/¼ pint extra virgin olive oil
4 tablespoons lemon juice
50 g/2 oz basil leaves, finely chopped
pinch of salt
pinch of cracked black peppercorns

1 First prepare the compote. Put the tomatoes, avocado, olive oil and lime juice into a bowl and add a dash each of Worcestershire and Tabasco sauces. Add salt and pepper to taste, cover and refrigerate until required.
2 To make the dressing, put all the ingredients into a screw-top jar and shake vigorously until combined.
3 Brush a heavy frying pan lightly with oil and warm over a high heat. Season the salmon fillets with salt and pepper, place flesh-side down in the pan and cook over a high heat for 2 minutes to brown the flesh. The fish should have a seared appearance.

4 Carefully transfer the fish, skin-side down, to a lightly oiled baking sheet. Transfer the baking sheet to a preheated oven at 240°C/475°F/Gas Mark 9 and cook for 7–9 minutes depending on thickness. To tell if the fish is cooked, take a peek inside it by slightly opening the flesh with a palette knife: if it is still pink, cook for a little longer. Don't forget, it will continue to cook after it has been removed from the oven.
5 Divide the compote between 4 large plates, arranging it in the centre of each one. Shake the dressing, then drizzle it over and around the compote. Set a piece of salmon on each mound of compote, garnish with basil leaves and serve immediately.

Peppered Tuna Steaks with Fennel, Red Onions and Sugar Snap Peas

Serves: **4**

Preparation time: 20–30 minutes

Cooking time: 30–40 minutes

4 tablespoons black peppercorns

1 teaspoon salt

4 trimmed tuna steaks, each weighing 125–150 g/4–5 oz, cut from the middle section of the fish

1 tablespoon olive oil

50 ml/2 fl oz brandy

150 ml/¼ pint concentrated fish or chicken stock

4 tablespoons lemon juice

50 g/2 oz unsalted butter, cut into small dice

150 ml/¼ pint double cream

2 tablespoons finely chopped parsley

4 flat leaf parsley sprigs, to garnish

VEGETABLES

2 fennel bulbs

2 red onions

125 g/4 oz sugar snap peas or mangetouts

4 potatoes

2 tablespoons olive oil

25 g/1 oz unsalted butter

1 First prepare the vegetables. Remove the feathery fronds from the fennel bulbs, chop finely and reserve. Trim the root ends off the fennel and discard. Cut the fennel in half lengthways and cut into 5 mm/¼ inch thick slices. Cut the onions into rings. Top and tail the sugar snaps or mangetouts and cut in half lengthways on the diagonal. Peel the potatoes.

2 Heat the oil and butter in a large pan, fry the fennel gently for 5 minutes, then add the onions. Cook over a moderate heat until the fennel and onions are tender, then increase the heat to colour slightly. Remove from the heat and keep warm. Boil the potatoes until just tender.

3 Meanwhile, coarsely crush the peppercorns with a pestle or the end of a rolling pin. Mix with the salt. Brush the tuna with the olive oil and press in the pepper mixture to coat them. Heat a large frying pan over a moderate heat. Set the steaks in the dry pan and fry for 2 minutes on one side, then turn and fry for 1 minute on the second side.

4 Add the sugar snaps or mangetouts to the fennel and onion mixture with the fennel fronds and toss over a high heat until hot. Drain the potatoes, cut each one into 4–5 slices and keep warm. Transfer the tuna to a warmed dish and keep warm.

5 Turn up the heat under the frying pan. Add any remaining cracked pepper, pour on the brandy and a little of the stock and stir to scrape up the sediment and any fish juices. Let the mixture bubble fiercely for a few seconds, then add the rest of the stock and the lemon juice and boil rapidly until syrupy.

6 Remove the pan from the heat and gradually add the butter pieces, stirring to combine them with the sauce and thicken it. Add the cream, still stirring to mix well. Bring to the boil for a few seconds, add the chopped parsley then reduce the heat. Keep warm while serving the fish.

7 Divide the vegetables between 4 warmed plates, arranging them in a mound in the centre. Set a tuna steak on top and pour over a little of the pepper sauce. Garnish each steak with a parsley sprig and serve immediately.

Fish in Wine Sauce

This delicately-flavoured Chinese dish is a classic that is not widely known. This is a pity because it is delicious and easy to make, ideal for the home cook.

Serves: **4**

Preparation time: 15 minutes

Cooking time: about 30 minutes

300–375 g/10–12 oz white fish fillets, skinned
1 egg white
2 garlic cloves, finely chopped
1 tablespoon cornflour
about 300 ml/½ pint groundnut oil, for
  deep-frying
salt and pepper
a few drops chilli oil, to serve
1 tablespoon chopped coriander leaves,
  to garnish
WINE SAUCE
250 ml/8 fl oz hot chicken stock
6 tablespoons Chinese rice wine or dry sherry
1 tablespoon cornflour
½ teaspoon sugar, or more to taste
2 tablespoons chopped coriander

1 Cut the fish into bite-sized pieces. Put the egg white and garlic into a bowl with salt and pepper to taste and whisk with a fork until frothy. Sift in the cornflour and whisk to mix, then add the fish pieces and stir until coated.

2 Heat the oil in a wok until very hot but not smoking. Deep-fry the fish in 4–6 batches for about 2 minutes per batch until crisp and light golden. Lift out with a slotted spoon and drain on kitchen paper. Very carefully pour off all the hot oil from the wok and wipe the wok clean with kitchen paper.

3 To make the sauce, pour the stock and rice wine or dry sherry into the wok and bring to the boil over a high heat. Blend the cornflour to a paste with a little cold water, then pour it into the wok and stir to mix. Simmer, stirring, for 2 minutes until thickened.

4 Add the sugar and stir to dissolve, then stir in the chopped coriander. Return the fish to the wok. Stir the fish very gently to coat it in the sauce and heat through for 1–2 minutes, then taste for seasoning and add more sugar if liked. Serve very hot with a few drops of chilli oil and garnished with coriander.

Sizzling Beef

Serves: **2–3**

Preparation time: about 15 minutes, plus freezing and marinating

Cooking time: about 20 minutes

1 piece of rump steak, weighing about
 375 g/12 oz, trimmed of all fat
5 cm/2 inch piece of fresh root ginger, peeled
 and grated
2 garlic cloves, crushed
1 tablespoon cornflour
2 teaspoons sugar
about 175 ml/6 fl oz groundnut oil, for
 deep-frying
150 g/5 oz carrots, cut into matchsticks
175 g/6 oz celery sticks, cut into matchsticks
175 ml/6 fl oz hot beef stock or water
1 tablespoon soy sauce
1–2 tablespoons chilli sauce, to taste
salt and pepper

1 Wrap the beef in clingfilm and place it in the freezer for 1–2 hours until it is just hard.
2 Remove the beef from the clingfilm and unwrap it, then slice it into very thin shreds, working against the grain. Place the shreds in a non-metallic dish, add the ginger, garlic, cornflour and half of the sugar and stir to mix. Leave to marinate at room temperature for about 30 minutes or until the beef is completely thawed out.
3 Heat the oil in a wok until very hot but not smoking. Add a small batch of beef strips and fry for 1–2 minutes or until the meat is browned on all sides. Stir the strips constantly during frying so they keep separate. Lift out with a slotted spoon and drain on kitchen paper. Repeat with the remaining beef.
4 Very carefully, pour off all but about 1 tablespoon of the hot oil from the wok. Add the carrots and stir-fry over high heat for 2 minutes, then add the celery and pour in the stock or water. Toss and stir-fry for about 4 minutes until the liquid has been absorbed by the vegetables.

5 Add the soy sauce and 1 tablespoon of the chilli sauce, then return all of the beef to the wok and sprinkle with the remaining sugar and salt and pepper to taste. Toss vigorously over the highest possible heat for 1–2 minutes until all the ingredients are shiny and sizzling. Taste and add more chilli sauce if liked. Serve very hot.

Crispy Lamb with Lettuce

Serves: **4–6**

Preparation time: 10 minutes, plus marinating and chilling

Cooking time: about 15 minutes

375 g/12 oz boneless lamb leg steaks or fillet
2 tablespoons soy sauce
1 tablespoon rice wine or dry sherry
2 garlic cloves, finely sliced

3 tablespoons cornflour
about 300 ml/½ pint groundnut oil, for frying
8–12 Cos lettuce leaves
4 spring onions, very finely shredded
¼ red pepper, cored, deseeded and finely diced,
 to garnish
TO SERVE
Chinese plum sauce
¼ red pepper, cored, deseeded and finely
 sliced (optional)

1 Cut the lamb across the grain into strips measuring about 5 cm/2 inches long and 1 cm/½ inch thick.
2 Put the soy sauce, rice wine or sherry and the garlic into a non-metallic dish and stir well to mix. Add the lamb and stir to coat, then cover the dish and leave to marinate in the refrigerator for at least 30 minutes.
3 Sift the cornflour over the lamb, mix into the meat and marinade. Put the lamb, uncovered, in the refrigerator for about 30 minutes.

4 Heat the oil in a wok until very hot but not smoking. Fry the marinated strips of lamb in about 4 batches for about 3 minutes per batch until they are crisp and browned all over. When cooked, lift out the pieces of lamb with a slotted spoon and set them aside to drain on kitchen paper.

5 To serve, arrange the lamb, lettuce and spring onions in separate dishes and garnish with finely diced red pepper. Let each person make their own parcels. The plum sauce should be spooned on to the lettuce, then the lamb and spring onions sprinkled on top and the lettuce wrapped around them.

Chicken with Sizzling Garlic

This is a simple dish with relatively few ingredients, but the garlic gives it a good flavour. It is pale in colour, so if you are going to serve it as part of a Chinese meal, the other dishes should be bright and colourful to achieve the correct balance.

Serves: **2–4**

Preparation time: 10–15 minutes, plus chilling

Cooking time: 15–20 minutes

2 boneless, skinless chicken breasts, total weight 250–300 g/8–10 oz

1 small egg

2 garlic cloves, crushed

about 4 tablespoons cornflour

about 175 ml/6 fl oz groundnut oil, for frying

salt and pepper

a few drops of chilli oil (optional), to serve

SAUCE

4 spring onions (white part only), finely shredded

2 garlic cloves, finely chopped

200 ml/7 fl oz hot chicken stock

4 tablespoons Chinese rice wine or dry sherry

1 teaspoon cornflour

TO GARNISH

½ tablespoon finely chopped red pepper

½ tablespoon finely chopped green pepper

finely shredded spring onion

1 Put the chicken breasts between clingfilm and pound with the base of a saucepan to flatten them. Remove the clingfilm and cut the chicken into strips about 2.5 cm/1 inch wide.

2 Beat the egg in a bowl with the crushed garlic and plenty of salt and pepper. Dip the chicken strips into the egg mixture, then place them in a single layer on a plate and dredge them with cornflour. Put the plate in the refrigerator for 30 minutes–1 hour, or longer if you have the time.

3 Heat the groundnut oil in a wok until very hot but not smoking. Immerse the chicken pieces in the hot oil one at a time until there are enough to fit in the pan in a single layer without overcrowding. Fry for about 3 minutes or until the chicken is golden, turning once. Remove with a slotted spoon and keep hot in a warmed bowl. Repeat with the remaining chicken.

4 Very carefully pour off all but about 1 teaspoon of the hot oil from the wok. Return the wok to a low heat and make the sauce. Put the spring onions, chopped garlic, stock and rice wine or sherry in the wok. Increase the heat to high and bring to the boil, stirring.

5 Blend the cornflour to a paste with a little cold water, then pour it into the wok and stir to mix. Simmer, stirring, for 1–2 minutes until the sauce thickens, then pour it over the chicken. Garnish with red and green pepper and the shredded spring onion, and sprinkle with a few drops of chilli oil, if liked. Serve at once.

Parsnip Duchesse Potatoes

Serves: **6**

Preparation time: 20 minutes

Cooking time: about 50 minutes

Oven temperature: 200°C/400°F/Gas Mark 6

750 g/1½ lb parsnips, cut into equal-sized pieces
750 g/1½ lb potatoes, cut into chunks
pinch of grated nutmeg
1 egg
salt and pepper

1 Cook the parsnips and potatoes in separate pans of salted boiling water for about 20 minutes, until tender.
2 Drain well, then mash together. Beat until smooth, then rub through a sieve. Turn the mixture into a bowl, season well with salt and pepper and beat in the nutmeg and egg.
3 Spoon the vegetable mixture into a piping bag fitted with a large star nozzle and pipe large whirls of the mixture on to a greased baking sheet.
4 Bake in a preheated oven at 200°C/400°F/Gas Mark 6 for about 25 minutes until lightly browned. Serve hot.

Baked Garlic with Brie

This classic Californian savoury can be accompanied by a wedge of Camembert, instead of the Brie. Make sure the cheese is nice and ripe for the best results. Serve this dish as a cheese course, or as a starter or light lunch, if preferred.

Serves: **4**

Preparation time: 5 minutes

Cooking time: 1¼ hours

Oven temperature: 200°C/400°F/Gas Mark 6

2 large garlic heads
150 ml/¼ pint extra virgin olive oil
2 rosemary sprigs, bruised
salt and pepper
TO SERVE
wedge of ripe Brie
crusty bread

1 Cut a small slice from the top of each head of garlic and sit the heads in a small baking tin. Pour over half the oil and top with the rosemary sprigs. Season well with salt and pepper, cover with foil and bake in a preheated oven at 200°C/400°F/Gas Mark 6 for 1 hour. Remove the foil, baste and bake for a further 15–20 minutes until caramelized.
2 Split each garlic head in two and then transfer each half to a small plate, drizzle over the remaining oil and serve with a wedge of Brie and plenty of crusty bread.

Pumpkin Pudding

Serves: **4**

Preparation time: 20 minutes, plus cooling

Cooking time: 50–55 minutes

Oven temperature: 190°C/375°F/Gas Mark 5

500 g/1 lb pumpkin, peeled, seeded and cubed
125 ml/4 fl oz cider
75 g/3 oz light brown sugar
¼ teaspoon mixed spice
50 g/2 oz butter
2 eggs, separated
50 g/2 oz sugar
2 tablespoons slivered almonds

1 Put the pumpkin cubes into a saucepan with the cider, brown sugar and mixed spice. Cover the pan and simmer gently until the pumpkin is tender.
2 Put the cooked pumpkin into a bowl and beat to a purée, then beat in the butter and egg yolks. Set aside to cool.
3 Whisk the egg whites until stiff. Whisk in the sugar. Fold the meringue lightly but thoroughly into the pumpkin mixture.
4 Spoon the pumpkin mixture into 4 large individual greased ramekins or a greased shallow ovenproof dish. Sprinkle with the slivered almonds. Bake in a preheated oven at 190°C/375°F/Gas Mark 5 for 30–35 minutes. Serve hot.

Chocolate and Raspberry Bombes

These pretty iced desserts take a little time to prepare, but can be made, decorated and stored in the freezer several days in advance.

Serves: **6**

Preparation time: 1 hour, plus cooling and freezing

Cooking time: 2 minutes

CHOCOLATE ICE CREAM
3 egg yolks
1 teaspoon vanilla essence
1½ teaspoons cornflour
50 g/2 oz caster sugar
175 g/6 oz plain chocolate, broken into pieces
300 ml/½ pint milk
300 ml/½ pint extra thick double cream
TO FINISH
500 g/1 lb good quality raspberry sorbet
50 g/2 oz plain chocolate, broken into pieces
5 g/¼ oz unsalted butter
TO DECORATE:
fresh raspberries
mint sprigs
icing sugar, for dusting

1 To make the ice cream, whisk the egg yolks, vanilla essence, cornflour and sugar in a bowl. Put the chocolate into a saucepan with the milk and heat gently, stirring, until the chocolate has melted. Pour over the egg mixture, whisking well.
2 Pour the mixture back into the saucepan and cook over a gentle heat, stirring, until slightly thickened. Pour into a bowl and cover the surface with greaseproof paper to prevent a skin forming. Leave to cool completely.
3 Whisk the cream into the cooled custard, then turn it into a freezer container. Freeze for several hours or overnight until firm.
4 Remove the ice cream from the freezer and leave it to soften for about 30 minutes. Put six 150 ml/¼ pint individual pudding moulds in the freezer for a few minutes until they are very cold.
5 Spread the softened ice cream around the base and sides of the moulds, leaving a cavity in the centre. Freeze until firm.
6 Leave the raspberry sorbet to soften at room temperature for about 30 minutes, then

pack it into the centre of each mould until level with the ice cream. Freeze until firm.

7 Dip each mould very briefly in hot water and twist until loosened. Tap out on to a freezerproof tray.

8 Put the chocolate into a small bowl with the butter and melt over a pan of simmering water. Place in a small piping bag fitted with a fine writing nozzle and scribble lines or loops of chocolate on to the ice creams. Alternatively, use a paper piping bag and snip off the tip.

9 Freeze the bombes until required, then transfer them to serving plates and decorate with raspberries, mint sprigs and a light dusting of icing sugar.

Chocolate Mousse

Serves: **4–6**

Preparation time: 10–12 minutes, plus chilling

4 eggs, separated
125 g/4 oz caster sugar
125 g/4 oz plain chocolate, broken into pieces
3 tablespoons water
300 ml/½ pint double cream
TO DECORATE
60 ml/2½ fl oz whipping cream, whipped
chocolate curls

1 Put the egg yolks and sugar into a bowl and whisk with an electric beater until thick and mousse-like.
2 Melt the chocolate with the water in a heatproof bowl set over a pan of simmering water. Remove from the heat and leave to cool slightly, then whisk into the egg mixture.
3 Whip the cream until it stands in soft peaks, then carefully fold it into the chocolate mixture. Whisk the egg whites until stiff, carefully fold 1 tablespoon into the mousse, then fold in the rest. Pour into 4–6 cups or small dishes and chill until set.
4 To serve, top each mousse with whipped cream, then make chocolate curls by shaving thin slivers from a bar of plain chocolate with a vegetable peeler.

Raspberry Meringue Cheesecake

Serves: **4**

Preparation time: 45 minutes, plus cooling and chilling

Cooking time: about 1¼ hours

Oven temperature: 150°C/300°F/Gas Mark 2

175 g/6 oz digestive biscuits, finely crushed
50 g/2 oz butter, melted
½ teaspoon ground cinnamon
FILLING
250 g/8 oz low-fat soft cheese
150 ml/¼ pint soured cream
1 teaspoon grated lemon rind
1 tablespoon lemon juice
1 teaspoon vanilla essence
75 g/3 oz caster sugar
1 egg, plus 2 egg yolks
FRUIT TOPPING
375 g/12 oz fresh raspberries or frozen
   raspberries, thawed
5 tablespoons redcurrant jelly
MERINGUE TOPPING
2 egg whites
125 g/4 oz caster sugar

1 Mix the biscuits with the melted butter and cinnamon. Press on to the bottom of 23 cm/9 inch flan dish. Leave the biscuit base in the refrigerator to set while you make the filling.
2 To make the filling, beat together the cheese and soured cream, then beat in the lemon rind, lemon juice, vanilla essence and sugar. Beat in the whole egg and egg yolks, and continue beating until the mixture is smooth.
3 Pour the filling over the biscuit base in the flan dish and bake in a preheated oven at 150°C/300°F/Gas Mark 2 for 1 hour or until the filling is set. Remove the cheesecake from the oven and leave to cool.
4 To make the fruit topping, arrange the raspberries in a single layer on the filling. Melt the jelly in a small saucepan and spoon it over the fruit. Allow the jelly to cool and set, then cover the cake with foil and chill in the refrigerator for at least 6 hours.
5 To make the meringue topping, whisk the egg whites until stiff. Whisk in half of the sugar and continue whisking until the mixture is stiff and glossy. Fold in the remaining sugar with a metal spoon. Spread the meringue carefully over the fruit so that it is completely covered – otherwise the jelly will melt. Level the top of the meringue.
6 Cook in a preheated oven at 180°C/350°F/ Gas Mark 4 for 10 minutes or until the meringue is golden brown. Serve immediately.

Ice-cream Cake

Serves: **4–6**

Preparation time: 20 minutes

Cooking time: 25 minutes

Oven temperature: 200°C/400°F/Gas Mark 6

3 eggs, separated
4 tablespoons hot water
175 g/6 oz caster sugar
¼ teaspoon vanilla essence
2 teaspoons finely grated orange rind
175 g/6 oz plain flour
50 g/2 oz cornflour
1 tablespoon baking powder
sifted icing sugar, to serve
FILLING
1.2 litres/2 pints vanilla ice cream
250 g/8 oz raspberries

1 Grease and baseline a 23 cm/9 inch round tin. Put the egg yolks, water, half the sugar, vanilla essence and orange rind into a large bowl and whisk until thick.
2 Sift the flour, cornflour and baking powder over the whisked mixture and fold in. In another bowl, whisk the egg whites until stiff, then slowly whisk in the remaining sugar. Fold into the flour mixture.
3 Turn the mixture into the prepared tin and bake in a preheated oven at 200°C/400°F/Gas Mark 6 for 25 minutes. Leave the cake in the tin for 5 minutes, then turn out and cool on a wire rack.
4 Slice the cake horizontally and sandwich together with the ice cream and raspberries. Sprinkle with icing sugar to serve.

Chestnut Roulade

Serves: **6–8**

Preparation time: 25 minutes

Cooking time: 25–30 minutes

Oven temperature: 180°C/350°F/Gas Mark 4

3 eggs, separated
125 g/4 oz caster sugar
250 g/8 oz can unsweetened chestnut purée
grated rind and juice of 1 orange
sieved icing sugar, for sprinkling
300 ml/½ pint double cream
2 tablespoons Grand Marnier or other orange liqueur
cocoa powder, for sprinkling

1 Whisk the egg yolks in a large bowl with the sugar until thick and creamy. Put the chestnut purée into another bowl with the orange juice and beat until blended, then whisk into the egg mixture. Whisk the egg whites until fairly stiff and fold in carefully. Turn into a greased and lined 30 x 20 cm/12 x 8 inch Swiss roll tin. Bake in a preheated oven at 180°C/350°F/Gas Mark 4 for 25–30 minutes, until firm.
2 Leave to cool for 5 minutes, then cover with a damp tea towel and leave until cold. Carefully turn the roulade on to a sheet of greaseproof paper sprinkled thickly with icing sugar. Peel off the lining paper.
3 Place the cream, grated orange rind and liqueur in a bowl and whip until stiff. Spread over the roulade and roll up like a Swiss roll. Serve sliced and sprinkled with cocoa powder.

The Perfect Host

Everyone wants to be the perfect host or hostess and everyone has their own idea of what exactly this means: welcoming, generous, tactful, interesting, witty, imaginative, charming, warm, unflappable, expansive, a brilliant cook, a good conversationalist and a skilled socialite. Unfortunately, however, few of us manage to be all these things all of the time, though most of us are still able to throw a successful and memorable party.

Above all other things, the perfect host wants his or her guests to have a thoroughly good time. He or she wants them to eat well, to feel comfortable and at their ease, to like meeting the other guests, to eat and drink their fill and, above all, to enjoy themselves.

But, as if by magic – and this is probably the more difficult part – this should appear to have happened almost by chance, almost accidentally, as if by luck rather than contrivance. Everything should be just so, but rather because it is always that way, not because any special trouble has been taken in honour of the occasion.

There should be absolutely no visible effort and no obvious sign of hard work, no suggestion of struggle or strain. It's almost as if the host might expect the guests to feel bad – guilty, perhaps, or at least uncomfortable – if they were able to discern any of the behind-the-scenes trickery and elbow grease or to guess at all the hard work that it must have cost their host to entertain them in such style.

As a result, the host/guest relationship is a slightly strange one. It's not an entirely straight one, and there's always the underlying recognition that there's been not a small element of dissembling. The effort must, of course, have been made – every guest expects that – but it must be totally invisible.

On Arrival

The first thing that the perfect host has to do is to greet his or her guests. And that means a lot more than just saying 'hello' – it's much more important than that; it also means expressing pleasure at seeing people and making them

feel welcome, important and wanted. Remember, the mood of the party starts at the front door.

If any of your guests have brought you a bunch of flowers, don't put this down and forget all about it, just because you're in a rush and you've got so many other things on your mind. You simply must find the time to put the flowers in water straight away, arrange them – albeit hurriedly – and place them somewhere for everyone to see. And if they've brought you chocolates, put these to one side – somewhere visible where you won't forget them, ready to offer round later with the coffee.

You also have to help your guests off with their coats and put them away somewhere convenient out of the way. This might simply be a matter of hanging them up in the hall cupboard – where you've cleared a space beforehand, of course – or putting them over a spare bed.

If these are the first guests to arrive, you must take them into the room and make them comfortable – which might be a question of asking them to sit down, if it's to be a sit-down party, or at least to stand somewhere comfortable. And then, of course, you should offer them their first drink.

It's amazing how quickly people relax once they've got a drink in their hands – though this is probably more to do with having been given something that symbolizes their welcome than the result of the alcohol itself. It may also be the result of having something to do with their hands, because it usually has much the same effect even when they're holding a non-alcoholic drink.

If there are already other guests present and people don't know each other, you must make the introductions, perhaps with a quick outline of who people are or what they do, which might give them an immediate lead into a conversational opening. Ideally, you should wait until they have started up some sort of conversation before leaving them to it, though this might not always be possible as the doorbell may ring again to announce the next arrivals.

If the guests are all old friends, the host will

probably be looking forward to a friendly evening of relaxed social interchange and reminiscences. But if people don't know each other, it's up to the host to behave as a discreet social broker. The host is not allowed to worry that the guests might not get on – after all, they've been hand picked specially for the event, haven't they? That is, of course, until one of your guests brings the friend from hell . . .

Staying Calm

No matter how calm you may feel before the event and no matter how determined you are to remain that way, there are a great many things that can go wrong and that can throw you off your guard. These fall, broadly speaking, into two categories: there are those that are your fault and for which you've got no one to blame but yourself; and there are those totally unforeseen and therefore out of your control.

These include the following:

A couple ring at the last minute to say that one of them has been taken ill and they can't come to dinner.

This completely throws out your numbers for dinner, your seating plan and the social interactions that you'd hoped for. What you can do about this rather depends on how much time you've got. If it's literally at the last minute, you'll probably have to rearrange your seating plan and make do. But if you've got time, you can ring someone else and ask them to come instead. You can only do this with really close and understanding friends who won't be offended to be asked to step in and make up the numbers at the last moment.

Someone doesn't turn up for dinner.

Rearrange your seating plan, take a deep breath and carry on as planned, vowing never to ask that person to dinner again, unless they have a very good excuse and they send you a huge bunch of flowers by way of apology. You may not end up with a lot of leftover food because people have a habit of simply ploughing their way through everything that is available, but if you do you can always freeze it (as long as none of it has already been frozen).

Someone brings a companion with them whom you don't like.

Above all, be tactful and don't allow your dislike for that person to show, nor your annoyance with the guest who brought him or her. Tact and discretion are two of a host's greatest qualities. Summon them now.

You forget to switch on the oven.

That should only mean a 15-minute delay or so, and all is not lost. Pour some more drinks, put out more nibbles to soak up the booze and carry on. Above all, stay calm and don't let your guests see you flustered.

You drop the main course on the floor.

You'll have to put your hand up to this one and confess. Providing people are having a good time, they can be surprisingly tolerant and understanding, particularly if they've had a few drinks. With a bit of luck, they'll see the funny side of the situation. There's not a lot you can do to salvage this situation, other than apologize and go to the takeaway.

The cat's sick all over the kitchen floor.

If possible, clear it up as discreetly and efficiently (using disinfectant) as possible so that your guests don't notice. If they do see, be as matter-of-fact as you can about it and don't make a fuss.

Worse still, the cat eats the fresh salmon, which was cooling on the kitchen table.

This is rather worse than being sick on the floor, and you may have to confess and resort

to the fish and chip shop! Alternatively, check in the freezer for anything that can be quickly cooked or reheated from frozen.

Someone spills a glass of red wine on the carpet.

Your guest will feel dreadfully guilty, so do everything you can to tell them not to worry – you have ways of removing red wine stains and it's not a problem. Then quickly pour some white wine over the fresh red wine or flush the area with a squirt from a soda siphon, and blot well. This will immediately neutralize the stain and make it easier to remove. Afterwards, attack the stain with carpet shampoo.

Your six-year-old develops a temperature of 40°C/104°F just half an hour before the guests are due to arrive.
You can hardly cancel at this point of the evening – some people are likely to be on their way. Your best bet is to make a quick telephone call to your doctor to describe symptoms and then administer paracetamol syrup, which will bring down your child's temperature and help him or her sleep. Make a regular check on your child throughout the evening – your guests will understand.

One of the guests gets drunk and starts being obstreperous and picking fights with the other guests.
It's difficult for a host to tell a guest to leave. If one of the other guests is a close friend, ask them to sort it out for you – calmly and discreetly – and to drive the difficult guest home or call a taxi. This should deal with some of the potential embarrassment.

Two of the guests have a row.
You'll probably all be able to laugh about this later but at the time, this situation can be disastrous. It calls upon your skills as a host, using all your tact to change the subject as discreetly and unobtrusively as possible and to deflect the argument.

Putting Guests at their Ease

If your guests are old friends, they will feel at home already, but if you don't know them well, or they don't know each other, they may feel uneasy at first. If you are having a large party, you will have to see to lots of things and lots of people all at once and one of your problems will be that of giving your divided attention to guests, while making each one feel like the most important person in the world.

There are several things that a host can do to put guests at their ease.
• smile a lot
• stay calm at all times
• be particularly sensitive to any very shy guests
• think of interests that guests have in common – mutual friends, schools (if guests have children) and the latest world news all being a good starting point – and guide the conversation round these
• never let people's glasses become empty
• arrange for guests to get a taxi home or, if they live too far away, ask them to stay the night. In this way, there will be no anxiety about guests driving home when they've been drinking.

Enjoy Yourself

All the guests are expected to have fun – that goes without saying. But the trick in the truly successful party is for the host to give the impression that he or she is also having as much fun as everyone else.

That means, in turn and inevitably, that the host must appear to be confident, relaxed, calm, untroubled, with not a care in the world. This is not, of course, always the case – far from it, in fact, though this depends very much on the specifics of the occasion.

One of the things that is most likely to put your guests at their ease is if you give the impression that you are enjoying yourself as much as they are. There are several ways in which you can do this:
• do as much advance preparation as you can
• make sure everything is ready in plenty of time
• don't panic
• don't rely on your memory but write a schedule of all the things you need to do on the night
• get yourself ready, too, so you look (and feel) good
• have a drink or two, by all means, but remember to stay sober and remain on top of the situation

Drunk Driving

The responsible party thrower will never ever let anyone drive home when they have been drinking. It's far better to let them stay the night or to call a taxi rather than let them take a chance on driving and endangering their own and other people's lives, as well as breaking the law. Be as persuasive as necessary in order to extract their keys from them. If they stay the night then there is no reason why the party can't continue for as long as everyone is enjoying themselves and the host can keep going. Alternatively there are also some enterprising firms that will send a car driver to your house on a small folding motorbike. The idea is that he puts his bike in the boot of the drinker's car and drives the drinker home in his own car. That way both car and drinker get home safely.

• always have a full glass of mineral water and sip regularly from it so that you appear to be drinking – your guests won't notice what!

RIGHT • A spilt glass of red wine is not the end of the world as long as it is dealt with straight away – be armed in advance with all the tools to cope with such accidents.

Index

A

Acceptances 31, 32
advance preparation 16–18, 154–5
al fresco parties 22–6, 152
  see also midsummer tea party
almonds
  briks 184
  honey cakes 194
  sweet biscotti 194
Americano, cocktail 136
anchovies
  anchoïade 180
  briks 184
  mini pissaladière 206
antipasto focaccia 202
apéritifs 115
  see also cocktails
apple posset, drinks 144
apricot brandy, cocktail 132
asparagus 54
  Parmesan and egg flan 212
  tuna teriyaki 228
atmosphere creation 10, 40–7,
  87–9
aubergine relish 186
  savoury samosas 184
avocado, compote 230

B

Baked garlic with Brie 238
baked ham, glazed 208
bands 26, 90
barbecues 24
bars, stocking & running 117, 120–2
basil and courgette soup 224
bathroom facilities 22, 42
Beaujolais Nouveau 114
beef, sizzling 234
beetroot crisps 176
Bellini, cocktail 138
Between the Sheets, cocktail 142
birthday parties 32, 44
biscuits
  with cheese 154
  cheese sablés 174
  shortbread 192
  sweet biscotti 194
black ear fungus, spring rolls 210
Black Russian, cocktail 130
black treacle, honey cakes 194
blenders, cocktail 119, 120–2
Blue Moon, cocktail 136
bottle openers 122
bottles used for wine 62
Bourbon whiskey, cocktails 132
brandy 115, 117
  mixing drinks 140, 144
Brandy Alexander, cocktail 142
brandy balloons 116
brandy snaps, midsummer tea
  party 68
bread 153
  antipasto focaccia 202
Brie with baked garlic 238
briks 184
broccoli, vegetables with Thai
  spiced coconut sauce 227
brunch parties 21
Buck's Fizz, cocktail 138
budgets 18, 21–2, 32, 61, 90
buffet menu suggestions 158–61
buffet parties
  planning 21, 31, 35, 72–5, 100, 152
  presentation 61, 87–9, 150
butter preparation 52

C

Cacti 55, 76
cakes 214–18, 244
Calvados, drinks 144
Camembert with baked garlic 238
Campari, cocktails 136
candles 24, 40, 44, 46, 50, 67, 72
candlesticks 46, 72
Caribbean fruit kebabs 214
carrot crisps 176
caterers 22, 61
catering, large numbers 156
celery, egg and cream cheese
  dip 186

cellars, wine storage 110
centrepieces 48–50, 72, 76
chair decorations 44
Champagne 104, 115
cocktails 138
  foods for 68–9, 108
  opening 113
  quantities per person 117
Champagne bottles 110
Champagne bubbles,
  preserving 114
Champagne flutes 116
Champagne towers 82, 113
Chavignol cheese with peppers
  and pine nuts 224
cheese
  anitpasto focaccia 202
  asparagus and egg flan 212
  baked garlic with Brie 238
  cheese and onion tartlets 212
  egg and celery dip 186
  goat's cheese with peppers and
    pine nuts 224
  Gorgonzola and walnut
    chicory 204
  ricotta parcels 172
  seeded cheese sablés 174
  spinach and ricotta puffs 202
  storing 154
  vol-au-vent filling 204
  wines for 108
cheese board, presentation 154
cheese course, timing 151–2
cheesecake 242
cherry brandy, cocktail 128
chestnut purée, marron
  meringues 216
chestnut roulade 244
chicken
  chicken saté 210
  chicken with sizzling garlic 236
  chicken wings, spiced 198
  savoury samosas 184
chickpeas, houmous 190
chicory, Gorgonzola and walnut 204
children, arrangements for 26,
  50, 70
chillies

cashew nuts toasted 178
chilli bean dip 190
chilli bean and pepper soup 222
chilli chips 172
  presentation 166
  scallops 228
  vegetables with Thai spiced
    coconut sauce 227
china, presentation 24, 46, 48,
  150, 162
China tea 74
Chinese dishes 72–5, 92, 234, 236
Chinese rice wine
  chicken with sizzling garlic 236
  scallops 228
  wine sauce 232
Chinese theme parties (see
  Oriental theme party)
chocolate
  chocolate cups 214
  chocolate ice cream 240
  chocolate mousse 242
  chocolate and raspberry
    bombes 240
chocolate sauce 214
  marshmallow crescents 192
  presentation 168
  profiteroles 218
  sweet biscotti 194
chocolates
  with coffee 124–5
  received 248
choux pastry 218
chowder, sweetcorn 222
christening party invitations 32
Christmas cake, tropical 218
Christmas parties 44, 158–61
chutney, mayonnaise 188
cinnamon, drinks 140
cleaning, preparation 25, 40
clearing-up 61–2
coats, arrangements for 40, 61, 248
Coca-cola, cocktails 132
cocktail blenders 119, 120–2
cocktail glasses 82, 116
cocktail parties 80–4, 87–9
  planning 37, 100, 158–61
cocktail shakers 80, 119, 120–2

cocktail sticks 122
cocktails 117–22
coconut, tropical Christmas
　　cake 218
coconut icing 218
coconut sauce 227
coffee 124–5
coffee liqueur, cocktails 130
Cointreau, cocktails 128, 136,
　　142, 144
Collinson, cocktail 128
compote, savoury 230
contingency plans 21, 24, 68
conversation 87, 89–90, 248
corkscrews 112–3, 122
corn and prawn fritters 178
Corpse Reviver 119
courgettes
　　courgette and dill soup 224
　　presentation 166
　　salmon and courgette
　　　brochettes 226
　　vegetables with Thai spiced
　　　coconut sauce 227
Cranberry Crush, drinks 146
cream cheese, egg and celery
　　dip 186
Crème de Cacao, cocktails 134, 142
Crème de Cassis 115, 138
Crème de Menthe, cocktails 134
crème fraîche, Gorgonzola and
　　walnut chicory 204
crisps 176
crispy lamb with lettuce 234
crispy ricotta parcels 172
crockery, presentation 28, 46, 48,
　　150, 162
Cuba Libre, cocktail 132
cucumber and mint raita 188
Curaçao, cocktails 136
cutlery 18, 24, 48, 50–1, 61, 150

D aiquiri, cocktail 134
dancing 22, 90
decanting wine 113

decorations 25, 40, 42–4, 48–50, 91
　　al fresco parties 24
　　for cocktails 122–3
　　Mexican dinner party 76–8
　　oriental buffet parties 72–5
　　sea world dinner parties 64–7
　　20s cocktail party 82
dessert, wines for 102, 108
dessert course, timing 151–2
digestifs 115
dill and courgette soup 224
dinner parties, planning 21, 30, 36,
　　42, 87–9, 100–4, 151–2, 158–61
dinner party table settings 48–54
dips
　　chilli bean dip 190
　　cream cheese, egg and
　　　celery 186
　　cucumber and mint raita 188
　　houmous 190
　　yellow pepper dip 198
disasters 248–50
dishes, presentation 28, 46, 48,
　　150, 162
disc jockeys, hiring 90
Drambuie, drinks 142
dress requirements 31–2
drinks 98–125
　　serving 25, 86, 248
drinks parties 21, 26, 31, 44, 100,
　　158–61
drinks planning 10, 18, 117
driving 100, 250
drunken guests 250
Dry Martini, cocktail 128
duchesse potatoes 238
duck, wines for 108
dumplings, potstickers 182

E dible decorations 72, 123,
　　162–7, 169, 178
eggs
　　asparagus and Parmesan cheese
　　　flan 212
　　briks 184

chocolate mousse 242
　　for cocktails 119, 122
　　egg and celery dip 186
　　meringues 216
　　polenta triangles 174
　　tropical Christmas cake 218
emergencies 42, 248–50
empties 62
entertainers, professional 26, 90–1
entertainment 84–97

F amily gatherings, music for
　　87–9
fancy dress 26, 72, 76
fennel, tuna steaks, red onions and
　　sugar snap peas 231
finger bowls 54
fire hazards 44, 46
first aid kit 42
fish, wines for 108
fish courses 152–4
fish in wine sauce 232
Florida Skies, cocktail 134
flowers 24–5, 40, 44–6, 48, 50, 61,
　　68, 70, 163
　　centrepieces 48–50
　　received 248
flute bottles 110
fontina bruschetta with
　　anchoïade 180
food preparation planning 10–12,
　　18, 150–4
food presentation 10, 61, 150,
　　162–9
food quantities per person 150–2
foods, with which wines 108
fortune cookies 92
French '75, cocktail 138
fritters 178
fruit
　　presentation 72, 122, 123,
　　　144, 164
　　wines for 108
fruit cups 86
fruit kebabs 214

Fruit Punch 146
furniture arranging 21, 25, 40, 42

G ame, wines for 108
games 92–6
garlic with Brie 238
garnishes 154, 162–7
gifts, received 248
gifts for guests 96–7
gin, cocktails 128, 138
ginger
　　drinks 146, 147
　　potstickers 182
　　scallops 228
　　spring rolls 210
　　yellow pepper dip 198
ginger & lime pickle
　　mayonnaise 188
ginger ale, drinks 147
ginger beer, cocktails 130
glasses
　　place settings 51
　　planning 18, 24, 48, 115, 115–7
glazed baked ham 208
globe artichokes 54
goat's cheese with peppers and
　　pine nuts 224
Gorgonzola and walnut chicory 204
Grand Marnier, drinks 140
grapes, vol-au-vent filling 204
Grasshopper, cocktail 134
green curry paste, coconut
　　sauce 227
green vegetables with Thai spiced
　　coconut sauce 227
grenadine, mixing drinks 132, 136,
　　138, 144, 147
grilled radicchio and fontina
　　bruschetta with anchoïade 180
guacamole 76
guest lists 18, 19, 21, 30–1

Ham
glazed baked 208
ricotta parcels 172
Harvey Wallbanger, cocktail 119
herbal tea 124
Highball glasses 116
hired help 22, 61, 156
honey cakes 194
hors d'oeuvre, wines for 108
hosting 12, 246–51
hot drinks, serving 119–10
houmous 190
housework 25, 40
Hurricane glasses 116

Ice 25, 117, 120, 162
ice-cream 70, 240
ice cubes, decorative for
cocktails 123
ice-cream cake 244
iced drinks, serving 119
impromptu parties 32
invitations 10, 28–37
Irish coffee 125

Japanese rice wine, teriyaki
sauce 228
Japanese tea 72
Japanese wine 72
Jarlsberg 153
jasmine tea 74

Kahlua coffee liqueur,
cocktails 130
karaoke 90
kebab-style dishes 210, 214, 226

kidney beans
chilli bean dip 190
chilli bean and pepper soup 222
Kir Royale, cocktail 138
kirsch, cocktails 128

Lamb with lettuce 234
leeks, savoury samosas 184
lemon juice, drinks 144
lemonade, drinks 142
lemons, drinks preparation 119,
138, 140
lettuce, crispy lamb with 234
lighting 24, 26, 40, 44–7, 74
lime juice
compote 230
drinks 134, 136, 144
limeade 147
limes
drinks preparation 119, 130,
132, 144
making juicy 147
liqueur glasses 116
liqueurs, quantities per person 117
lists, preparing 18, 152, 156, 250
live musicians 86, 90
lumpfish roe, Russian potatoes 200

Mangetouts, vegetables
with Thai spiced coconut
sauce 227
mangoes, drinks 144
Manhattan, cocktail 123
Margarita, cocktail 136
Margarita glasses 80, 116
marinades 198, 210, 226
marron meringues 216
marshmallow crescents 192
mascarpone, vol-au-vent filling 204
mayonnaise, ginger & lime
pickle 188
measures 4

bar drinks 122
meat, wines for 108
menu cards for the table 50
menu planning 18, 158–61
meringues 242
marron 216
Mexican theme parties 36, 40, 52,
55–6, 76–9
midsummer tea parties 34, 44, 49,
68–71
mineral water, quantities per
person 117
mini pissaladière 206
mint, cucumber raita 188
Mint Julep, cocktail 132
mixers 117
mixing glass 120
mocha icing 218
mood creation 10, 40–7, 87–9
Moscow Mule, cocktail 130
mousse, chocolate 242
mozzarella cheese
antipasto focaccia 202
polenta triangles 174
mulled wine 40, 140
serving 119
mushrooms, vol-au-vent filling 204
music 86, 87–9
Mexican dinner party 76
midsummer tea party 68
sea world dinner parties 64–7
20s cocktail party 80
musicians, live 26, 86, 90

Napkins 24, 52–3, 58–9,
61, 78
neighbours 18, 21, 90
nibbles, serving 86, 150
non-alcoholic drinks 100, 117
noodles, spring rolls 210
nose, wines 106
numbers of guests 21, 30, 31

Old-fashioned glasses 116
olives
mini pissaladière 206
vol-au-vent filling 204
onion and cheese tartlets 212
onions, mini pissaladière 206
orange bitters, cocktails 128
Orange Blossom, cocktail 128
orange cakes 216
orange juice 115, 117
chocolate cups 214
cocktails 128, 130, 136, 138,
142, 146
oranges 123, 140, 144, 165
Oriental theme parties 35, 42, 59,
72–5, 89

Parmesan cheese
asparagus and egg flan 212
palmiers 176
polenta triangles 174
sablés 174
parsnip crisps 176
parsnip duchesse potatoes 238
party planners 61, 90
pastry dishes 172, 176, 184, 202,
204, 206, 212
pastry doughs 206, 212, 218
peas
tuna steaks, fennel and red
onions 231
vegetables with Thai spiced
coconut sauce 227
peppered tuna steaks with fennel,
red onions and sugar snap
peas 231
peppers
chilli bean dip 190
chilli bean and pepper soup 222
crispy lamb with lettuce 234
goat's cheese with peppers and
pine nuts 224

presentation 166
    vol-au-vent filling 204
    yellow pepper dip 198
perfume from flowers 44
Pernod, cocktails 132
petits fours 124–5
pickle, mayonnaise 188
picnics 24, 110, 158–61
Pilsner glasses 116
Pina Colada, cocktail 134
pine nuts
    anchoïade 180
    goat's cheese with peppers and
        pine nuts 224
pineapple
    fruit kebabs 214
    tropical Christmas cake 218
pineapple juice
    cocktails 132, 134
    drinks 146
place names 54, 76–7
place setting rules 50–1
planning 8–10, 14–27, 25–6
    drinks 100–4
    hired help duties 61
    menus 10–12, 18, 158–61
Planter's Punch 119
polenta triangles 174
pork
    spring rolls 210
    wines for 108
port, mulled red wine 140
potatoes 172
    chips 172
    crisps 176
    duchesse 238
    Russian 200
    savoury samosas 184
    sweetcorn chowder 222
potstickers 182
poultry, wines for 108
prawn and corn fritters 178
prawns, potstickers 182
prawns with plum sauce 200
preparations 25, 38–63
presentation 40, 82, 123, 162–9
problems 248–50
profiteroles 218

Prohibition 117–19
pumpkin pudding 240
punch bowls 81
punches 86

Quantities, calculating 117,
    150–2

Radicchio and fontina
    bruschetta with anchoïade 180
raspberry and chocolate
    bombes 240
raspberry meringue
    cheesecake 242
ravanie 216
Red Leicester cheese and onion
    tartlets 212
red onions, tuna steaks, fennel and
    sugar snap peas 231
red wine 142, 144
    mulled 140
red wine stain removal 42, 249
redcurrants, presentation 164
rice wine
    chicken with garlic sauce 236
    crispy lamb with lettuce 234
    scallops 228
    teriyaki sauce 228
    wine sauce 232
ricotta cheese, spinach and ricotta
    puffs 202
ricotta parcels 172
roast fillet of salmon 230
rocket, presentation 166
roe, Russian potatoes 200
root vegetable crisps 176
Rosé Cup, drinks 140
rosé wines, foods for 108
roulade 244
rubbish arrangements 22, 24
rum
    chocolate sauce 214

cocktails 132, 142
    drinks 140
rum cocktails 134
Russian potatoes 200

Salami, antipasto focaccia 202
salmon, roast fillet 230
salmon and courgette
    brochettes 226
Sangria, drinks 144
saté sauce 210
sauces 210
    chicken with garlic 236
    chocolate with rum 214
    coconut 227
saté 210
    teriyaki 228
    wine 232
savoury samosas 184
savoury vol-au-vents 204
scallops 228
scene setting 10, 38–63, 87–9
schedules 18, 152, 156, 250
Scotch whisky, cocktails 132
Screwdriver, cocktail 130
sea world theme parties 33, 47, 53,
    56, 64–7
seating arrangements 21, 22–4,
    42, 54
seeded cheese sablés 174
semolina, ravanie cakes 216
serving wine 114–17
sherry
    chicken with garlic sauce 236
    crispy lamb with lettuce 234
sweetcorn chowder 222
    wine sauce 232
shooters 119
shortbread 192
Siamese Slammer, drinks 144
Sichuan scallops 228
Singapore Sling, cocktail 128
sizzling beef 234
smoked ham, ricotta parcels 172
smoking 22, 124

soda water 117, 132, 134, 136, 140,
    144, 146
soft drinks, quantities per
    person 117
soup, wines for 108
soups 222–4
Southern Comfort, drinks 140
space per person 21, 42
spare ribs 54
sparkling white wine, cocktails 138
sparkling wines 104, 115
special occasions 16, 32, 158–61
spiced chicken wings 198
spiced coconut sauce 227
spicy palmiers 176
spinach
    ricotta parcels 172
    savoury samosas 184
spinach and ricotta puffs 202
spirits, quantities per person 117
spring rolls 210
strawberries 68–9, 147
    fruit kebabs 214
street parties 21
sugar snap peas, tuna steaks,
    fennel and red onions 231
sugar syrup 122
Summer Cup, drinks 142
sun-dried tomatoes, antipasto
    focaccia 202
supper menu suggestions 158–61
sweet biscotti 194
sweet and sour aubergine
    relish 186
sweetcorn, fritters 178
sweetcorn chowder 222
syrup glaze 216
syrups, for cocktails 122

Table linen 46
table settings 22–4, 25, 42, 46,
    48–54, 65–7
    rules 50–1
tableware, hiring 61
tahini paste, houmous 190

talking 87, 89–90, 248
tasting wines 106–7
taxis 42, 250
tea 124
tea parties 26, 34, 68–71, 158–61
Tea Punch, drinks 140
temperature, wines 110, 114
Tenderberry, drinks 147
tequila, drinks 144
Tequila Sunrise, cocktail 136
teriyaki sauce 228
Thai red curry paste, prawn
    fritters 178
Thai spiced coconut sauce 227
Thai Sunrise, drinks 144
theme parties 26, 33–7, 62–83,
    87–9, 90–1
Tia Maria, cocktails 130
time planning 19, 21, 25–6, 31–2
timetables 156
tomatoes
    briks 184
    compote 230
    sun-dried, antipasto
        focaccia 202
tonic water, drinks 140
tortillas 76
traditional shortbread 192
tropical Christmas cake 218
trouble shooting 248–50
tuna steaks with fennel, red onions
    and sugar snap peas 231
tuna teryaki 228
turnovers, briks 184
20s cocktail party 80–4

V

Vegetable crisps 176
vegetables with Thai spiced
    coconut sauce 227
venue planning 19, 21–4, 31–2
vermouth, cocktails 128, 136
Vietnamese spring rolls 210
vinaigrette 224
vodka, cocktails 130, 136, 144

W

Walnut and Gorgonzola
    chicory 204
walnuts, tropical Christmas
    cake 218
washing up 61–2
wedding invitations 32
welcomes 40, 86, 248, 250
whisky, mulled white wine 140
Whisky Daisy, cocktail 132
White Russian, cocktail 130
white wine 140, 142
wine
    opening 112
    quantities per person 117
wine bottles, types of 110
wine boxes 110
wine coolers 120
wine sauce 232
    choosing 100–9
    learning about 104–8
    serving 114–17
    storing 110
    which with foods 108
winter celebration meal menu
    suggestions 158–61
wok dishes 178, 182, 228, 232,
    234, 236
wonton wrappers 182
Worcestershire Sauce 117
wrappings, for gifts 96–7
written invitations 31–2

Y

Yellow pepper dip 198
yogurt
    cucumber and mint raita 188
    Russian potatoes 200
    yellow pepper dip 198

Z

Zombie, cocktail 132

Acknowledgments

Special photography: Bill Reavell

Other photography: Octopus Publishing Group Ltd/Jean Cazals 17, 22, 42, 96 left, 102, 103, 104, 105, 106 left, 106 right, 107, 109, 111, 112, 114 left, 114 right, 148, 153, 154, 169, 248/Anna Hodgson 50, 51, 54, 60/Sandra Lane 7, 9, 11, 19 top, 20, 63, 98, 115, 118, 121, 162, 163, 164, 167/Neil Mersh 116/Peter Myers 13, 24–25, 119, 124, 125 top, 125 bottom, 168/Sean Myers 166/Bill Reavell 18, 27, 28, 30, 31 left, 33 top Left, 33 top right, 33 bottom, 34 right, 34 top left, 34 bottom left, 35 right, 35 top left, 35 bottom left, 36 right, 36 top left, 36 bottom left, 37 right, 37 top left, 37 bottom left, 38, 40, 41, 43, 44, 45, 46, 47 right, 47 top left, 47 bottom left, 48, 49, 52 bottom, 53 top, 53 bottom, 55 right, 55 top left, 55 bottom left, 56 right, 56 top left, 56 bottom left, 57 right, 57 top left, 57 bottom left, 58 right, 58 top left, 58 bottom left, 59 right, 59 top left, 59 bottom left, 64 top, 64 bottom, 65 left, 65 right, 66 top, 66 bottom, 67, 68 top, 68 bottom, 69 top left, 69 top right, 69 bottom, 70 top, 70 bottom, 71, 72 top, 72 bottom, 73 left, 73 right, 74 top, 75, 76 top, 76 bottom, 77 left, 77 right, 78 top, 78 bottom left, 78 bottom right, 79, 80 top, 80 bottom, 81, 82 top, 82 top right, 82 bottom, 84, 86, 87, 88, 89, 92, 93, 94, 95, 96 right, 97 right, 97 top left, 97 bottom left, 101, 113, 120 left, 120 right, 122, 123 top, 123 bottom left, 123 bottom right, 126-127, 128, 129, 131, 132, 133, 134, 135, 136, 137, 138, 139, 140, 141, 142, 143, 144, 145, 146, 147, 155, 156, 158, 165, 246.

Special Photography Home Economist: Steven Wheeler